cook's practical handbook:
bread machine

essential tips and techniques for your bread machine,
including over 50 fabulous recipes

jennie shapter

LORENZ BOOKS

This edition is published by Lorenz Books

Lorenz Books is an imprint of Anness Publishing Ltd
Hermes House, 88–89 Blackfriars Road, London SE1 8HA

tel. 020 7401 2077; fax 020 7633 9499
www.lorenzbooks.com; info@anness.com
© Anness Publishing Ltd 2001, 2003

UK agent: The Manning Partnership Ltd, 6 The Old Dairy, Melcombe Road, Bath BA2 3LR;
tel. 01225 478444; fax 01225 478440; sales@manning-partnership.co.uk

UK distributor: Grantham Book Services Ltd, Isaac Newton Way, Alma Park Industrial Estate, Grantham, Lincs NG31 9SD;
tel. 01476 541080; fax 01476 541061; orders@gbs.tbs-ltd.co.uk

North American agent/distributor: National Book Network, 4501 Forbes Boulevard, Suite 200, Lanham, MD 20706;
tel. 301 459 3366; fax 301 429 5746; www.nbnbooks.com

Australian agent/distributor: Pan Macmillan Australia, Level 18, St Martins Tower, 31 Market St, Sydney, NSW 2000;
tel. 1300 135 113; fax 1300 135 103; customer.service@macmillan.com.au

New Zealand agent/distributor: David Bateman Ltd, 30 Tarndale Grove, Off Bush Road, Albany, Auckland;
tel. (09) 415 7664; fax (09) 415 8892

A CIP catalogue record for this book is available from the British Library.

Publisher: Joanna Lorenz
Managing Editor: Linda Fraser
Editor: Rebecca Clunes
Designer: Nigel Partridge
Photographer and Stylist: Nicki Dowey
Home Economist: Jennie Shapter
Production Controller: Yolande Denny

Previously published as Bread Machine Basics

1 3 5 7 9 10 8 6 4 2

Notes

Bracketed terms are intended for American readers. American terms are only given in the list of ingredients for
the small size of bread machine: please refer to this ingredients list if you are making bread in a larger machine.

The recipes in this book have all been written and tested for use in a variety of bread machines
available from leading manufacturers. For best results, refer to your manufacturer's handbook to confirm the
proportion of flour to liquids. You may need to adjust the recipes to suit your machine.

For all recipes, quantities are given in both metric and imperial measures and, where appropriate, measures are
also given in standard cups and spoons. Follow one set, but not a mixture, because they are not interchangeable.
In particular, metric/imperial measures and cup conversions are not consistent in order to accommodate the differences
in absorption of different flours.

Standard spoon and cup measures are level. 1 tsp = 5ml, 1 tbsp = 15ml, 1 cup = 235ml/8fl oz
Australian standard tablespoons are 20ml. Australian readers should use 3 tsp in place
of 1 tbsp for measuring small quantities of ingredients.

Medium (US large) eggs are used unless otherwise stated.

CONTENTS

INTRODUCTION

In recent years there has been a huge upsurge in the popularity of home-baked bread. Men and women are coming home from work to the comforting aroma of freshly baked bread once only associated with an idyllic childhood. But making and eating home-baked bread is not only the stuff of dreams. No. The bread that stands cooling in many of our kitchens is real. It has a beautiful golden crust, an even crumb and a delicious flavour. It

BELOW: To many people, a Farmhouse Loaf is the traditional bread they associate with their childhood.

looks and tastes as if aching effort went into its making, but nothing could be further from the truth. Much of today's tastiest bread is made at home with the aid of an easy-to-operate machine, which takes the hard work out of bread making while retaining all the pleasure.

The first automatic domestic bread-maker appeared on the market in Japan in the late 1980s, and since then bread machines have gained popularity all over the world. These excellent appliances have helped to rekindle the pleasure of making home-made bread, by stream-lining the process and making it incredibly

simple. All the "home baker" needs to do is to measure a few ingredients accurately, put them into the bread machine pan and push a button or two.

At first, it is easy to feel overwhelmed by all the settings on a bread machine. These are there to help you bake a wide range of breads, both sweet and savoury, using different grains and flavourings. In time, you'll understand them all, but there's no need to rush. Start by making a simple white loaf and watch while your machine transforms a few ingredients first into a silky, smooth dough and finally into a golden loaf of bread.

No matter what make of machine you have, it is important to focus on the bread, not the machine. Even the best type of machine is only a kitchen aid. The machine will mix, knead and bake beauti-fully, but only after you have added the necessary ingredients and programmed it. The machine cannot think for itself; it can only carry out your instructions, so it is essential that you add the correct ingre-dients in the right proportions, in the order specified in the instructions for your particular breadmaking machine, and that you choose the requisite settings. Do not become frustrated if your first attempts do not look one hundred per cent perfect; they will probably still taste wonderful. Get to know your bread machine and be willing to experiment to find the correct ratio of dry ingredients to liquids. There are a number of variables, including the type of ingredients used, the climate and the weather, which can affect the moisture level, regardless of the type of machine you are using.

When you make bread by hand you can feel whether it is too wet or dry, simply by kneading it. However, when you use a bread machine, you need to adopt a dif-ferent strategy to determine if your bread has the right moistness and, if not, how you may adjust it to produce a perfect loaf.

After the machine has been mixing for a few minutes, take a quick look at the dough – it should be pliable and soft. When the machine stops kneading, the

dough should start to relax back into the shape of the bread machine pan. Once you have made a few loaves of bread, you will soon recognize what is an acceptable dough, and you will rapidly progress to making breads with different grains, such as rye, buckwheat or barley, or breads flavoured with vegetables, such as potatoes or courgettes (zucchini). The range of both savoury and sweet breads you will be able to produce will be limited only by your imagination. Creative thinking can produce some magical results.

The breads in this book are either made entirely by machine or the dough is made in the machine, then shaped by hand and baked in a conventional oven. Teabreads are mixed by hand and baked in the bread machine. Where the loaves are made automatically, you will usually find three separate lists of ingredients, each relating to a different size of machine. The small size is recommended for bread machines that are designed for loaves using 350–375g/12–13oz/3–3¼ cups of flour, the medium size for machines that make loaves using 450–500g/1lb–1lb 2oz/4–4½ cups of flour and the large size for bread machines that are capable of making loaves using up to

BELOW: Mix the dough for Pistolets in the machine and shape by hand.

ABOVE: Babka is a traditional Polish Easter cake.

675g/1½lb/6 cups of flour. Refer to your manufacturer's handbook if you are not sure of the capacity of your machine. If only one set of ingredients is given for a loaf that is to be baked automatically, relate these to the size of your machine to make sure it is suitable for the job.

Where a bread machine is used solely for preparing the dough, which is then shaped by hand and baked conventionally, quantities are not so crucial, and only one set of ingredients is given.

It is very pleasurable to shape your own loaves of bread, and setting the machine to the "dough only" cycle takes all the hard work out of the initial mixing and kneading. The machine provides an ideal climate for the initial rising period, leaving you to bring all your artistry to bear on transforming the dough into rolls, shaped breads or yeast cakes. Once you master the technique, you can make breads from all around the world, including French Bread, American Breakfast Pancakes, Wholemeal English Muffins and Danish Pastries – to name but a few. Traditional breads, made to celebrate special occasions, can also be made in a bread machine. Try the classic Easter breads such as Easter Tea Ring or Polish Babka. It is also possible to make gluten-free breads, but as this is a specialist area, it is best to follow the instructions given by your manufacturer, or contact their helpline, if you wish to do this.

A BAKERY IN YOUR KITCHEN

Bread making is a tremendously satisfying activity. With the help of your machine, delectable breads you will not find at the bakery or supermarket can be made with very little effort. From basic breads containing little more than flour, yeast and water to more elaborate loaves based on stoneground flours milled from a variety of grains – the possibilities are endless. What's more, you know precisely what goes into the bread, and can tailor loaves to your family's own tastes, adding sweet or savoury ingredients.

For everyday use, basic white loaves, possibly enriched with milk or egg, or tasty multigrain and Light Wholemeal Breads are perfect for breakfast, whether freshly baked or toasted, and these can also be used for sandwiches and quick snacks. These types of bread are the easiest to make in your machine and are the ones you are likely to make over and over again. In time, however, you will probably progress to baking loaves with added ingredients, such as potato, to provide, for example, an enhanced lightness to the dough. Leftover rice makes a tasty bread; and other delicious treats are Sweet Potato Bread, a colourful, moist loaf with a rich golden crust, and Sun-dried Tomato Bread, full of Mediterranean flavours.

ABOVE: Hazelnut Twist Cake

BELOW: Strawberry Teabread

With the addition of other grains, you can make more complex, hearty loaves. Breads containing oats, rye, wheatgerm and wild rice, perhaps with added whole seeds and grains, can all be baked in the bread machine. These provide extra fibre and are a good source of complex carbohydrates, and are thus a wonderfully healthy option as well as being simply scrumptious. Try the delicious Barley-enriched Farmhouse Loaf, a healthy, flavour-packed loaf made from wheat and barley flours with pumpkin or sunflower seeds. Alternatively, experiment with a Malted Loaf, packed with flavoursome malt extract and dried fruit, making it both tasty and very nutritious.

The bread machine will happily incorporate such ingredients as caramelized onions, sun-dried tomatoes, chargrilled (bell) peppers, crispy bacon, slivers of ham and other cured meats, chopped fresh herbs and grated or crumbled cheese, to produce mouthwatering vegetable and other savoury breads. Spices and nuts, and dried, semi-dried and fresh fruits can also be added to make classic malted fruit loaves. Try succulent Apricot, Prune and Peach Teabread or Banana and Pecan Teabread. Other sweet breads include crunchy Buckwheat and Walnut Bread and that classic family favourite, Gingerbread.

You can also cook succulent teabreads, Treacle, Date and Walnut Cake, Peanut Butter Teabread and Coconut Cake to name but a few, a good alternative to using your traditional oven for one cake. Fresh fruits such as strawberries and raspberries plus more exotic offerings can also be used as flavourings for these afternoon treats, as can traditional dried fruits, such as apricots, dates, prunes and raisins.

These breads, mixed, proved and baked automatically, illustrate just a part of the bread machine's capabilities. You

BELOW: A flavoured bread, such as Grainy Mustard and Beer Loaf, is delicious served with cheese and pickle as a simple lunch.

can also use the "dough only" setting to make an endless variety of doughs for hand-shaping. Classic French Bread or rustic breads, such as Mixed Herb Cottage Loaf and Three Cheeses Bread are all possible, as are Italian breads, such as Stromboli, a variation on focaccia, and Mocha Panettone – without which, no traditional Italian Christmas would be considered complete.

Sweet yeast doughs work well in a bread machine. Try making Rum and Raisin Loaf and Mixed Peel Braid, as well as classic festive breads such as Polish Babka or Easter Tea Ring.

There are endless shaped rolls, buns and pastries to try out, from American Breakfast Pancakes to English Chelsea Buns, and from Italian Ricotta and Oregano Knots to Apple and Sultana Danish Pastries. For a special treat and every chocolate lover's dream, try Petit Pain au Chocolat, melt-in-the-mouth crisp, yeast pastry rolls filled with chocolate. Whether savoury or sweet, all these breads and rolls can be easily shaped by hand – after the machine has taken away the hard work of mixing and has proved (risen) the dough – and then baked to golden perfection in a conventional oven.

GETTING DOWN TO BASICS

A bread machine is designed to take the hard work out of making bread. Like most kitchen appliances, it is a labour-saving device. It will mix the ingredients and knead the dough for you, and allows the bread to rise and bake at the correct time and temperature.

For most breads, all you will need to do is to measure the ingredients for your chosen bread, put them into the pan in the correct order, close the lid, select a suitable baking programme and opt for light, medium or dark crust. You may also choose to delay the starting time, so that you have freshly baked bread for breakfast or when you return from work. Press the Start button and in a few hours you will have a beautifully baked loaf, the machine having performed the kneading, rising and baking cycles for you.

Bread machines offer a selection of programmes to suit different types of flour and varying levels of sugar and fat. You can explore making a whole variety of raw

BELOW: The three different sizes of bread machine pans that are available. From left to right: large, small and medium.

ABOVE: The shape of the kneading blade varies among different models of bread machine.

doughs for shaping sweet and savoury breads, sourdough breads, mixed-grains, Continental-style breads and many more.

All bread machines work on the same basic principle. Each contains a removable non-stick bread pan, with a handle, into which a kneading blade is fitted. When inserted in the machine, the pan fits on to a central shaft, which rotates the blade. A lid closes over the bread pan so that the ingredients are contained within a controlled environment. The lid includes an air vent and may have a window, which can be useful for checking the progress of your bread. The machine is programmed by using the control panel.

The size and shape of the bread is determined by the shape of the bread pan. There are two shapes currently available; one rectangular and the other square. The rectangular pan produces the more traditional shape, the actual size varying from one manufacturer to another. The square shape is mostly to be found in smaller machines and produces a tall loaf, which is similar to a traditional rectangular loaf that has been stood on its end. The vertical square loaf can be turned on its side for slicing, if preferred, in order to give smaller slices of bread.

The size of the loaf ranges from about 500g/1lb 2oz to 1.4kg/3lb, depending on the machine, with most large machines offering the option of baking smaller loaves as well. One machine will make small, medium and large loaves.

BUYING A BREAD MACHINE

There is plenty of choice when it comes to selecting a bread machine to buy. Give some thought to which features would prove most useful to you, then shop around for the best buy available in your price range. First of all, consider the size

of loaf you would like to bake, which will largely be governed by the number in your family. Remember that a large bread machine will often make smaller loaves but not vice versa.

You will need to consider whether the shape of the bread is important to you, and choose a machine with a square or rectangular bread pan accordingly.

Are you likely to want to make breads with added ingredients? If so, a raisin beep is useful. Does the machine have speciality flour cycles for whole wheat loaves? Would this matter to you? Another feature, the dough cycle, adds a great deal of flexibility, as it allows you to make hand-shaped breads. Extra features, such as jam-making and rice-cooking facilities, are very specialized and only you know whether you would find them worth having.

One important consideration is whether the manufacturer offers a well-written manual and an after-sales support system or help line. If these are available, any problems or queries you might have can be answered quickly, which is particularly useful if this is your first machine.

A bread machine takes up a fair amount of room, so think about where you will store it, and buy one that fits the available space. If the bread machine is to be left on the work surface and aesthetics are important to you, you'll need to buy a machine that will be in keeping with your existing appliances. Most bread machines are available in white or black, or in stainless steel.

Jot down the features important to you, listing them in order of your preference. Use a simple process of elimination to narrow your choice down to two or three machines, which will make the decision easier.

BELOW: A typical bread machine. Although each machine will have a control panel with a different layout, most of the basic features are similar. More specialist cycles vary from machine to machine.

BUILT-IN SAFETY DEVICES

Most machines include a power failure override mode which can prove to be extremely useful. If the machine is inadvertently unplugged or there is a brief power cut, the programme will continue as soon as the power is restored. The maximum time allowed for loss of power varies from 10 to 30 minutes. Check the bread when the power comes back on; depending on what stage the programme had reached at the time of the power cut, the rising or baking time of the loaf may have been affected.

An over-load protection is fitted to some models. This will cut in if the kneading blade is restricted by hard dough and will stop the motor to protect it. It will automatically re-start after about 30 minutes, but it is important to rectify the problem dough first. Either start again or cut the dough into small pieces and return it to the bread pan with a little more liquid to soften the dough.

HOW TO USE YOUR BREAD MACHINE

The instructions that follow will help you to achieve a perfect loaf the first time you use your bread machine. The guidelines are general, that is they are applicable to any bread machine, and should be read in conjunction with the handbook provided for your specific machine. Make sure you use fresh, top quality ingredients; you can't expect good results with out-of-date flour or yeast.

1 Stand the bread machine on a firm, level, heat-resistant surface. Place away from any heat source, such as a stove or direct sunlight, and also in a draught-free area, as these factors can affect the temperature inside the machine. Do not plug the bread machine into the power socket at this stage. Open the lid. Remove the bread pan by holding both sides of the handle and pulling upwards or twisting slightly, depending on the design of your particular model.

2 Make sure the kneading blade and shaft are free of any breadcrumbs left behind when the machine was last used. Fit the kneading blade on the shaft in the base of the bread pan. The blade will fit only in one position, as the hole in the blade and the outside of the shaft are D-shaped.

3 Pour the water, milk and/or other liquids into the bread pan, unless the instructions for your particular machine require you to add the dry ingredients first. If so, reverse the order in which you add the liquid and dry ingredients, putting the yeast in the bread pan first.

4 Sprinkle over the flour, ensuring that it covers the liquid completely. Add any other dry ingredients specified in the recipe, such as dried milk powder. Add the salt, sugar or honey and butter or oil, placing them in separate corners so they do not come into contact with each other.

SPECIAL FEATURES

Extra programmes can be found on more expensive machines. These include cooking jam or rice and making pasta dough. While these facilities would not be the main reason for buying a bread machine they can be useful extras. For instance, jam-making couldn't be easier: you simply add equal quantities of fresh fruit and sugar to the bread machine pan, set the jam programme and, when the cycle ends, you will have jam ready to pour into clean sterilized jars.

EASY MEASURING

If you have a set of electronic scales with an add and weigh facility, then accurate measuring of ingredients is very easy. Stand the bread pan on the scale, pour in the liquid, then set the display to zero. Add the dry ingredients directly to the pan, each time zeroing the display. Finally, add the fat, salt, sweetener and yeast and place the bread pan in your machine.

5 Make a small indent in the centre of the flour (but not down as far as the liquid) with the tip of your finger and add the yeast. If your indent reached the liquid below the dry ingredients, then the yeast would become wet and would be activated too quickly. Wipe away any spillages from the outside of the bread pan.

6 Place the pan inside the machine, fitting it firmly in place. Depending on the model of your machine, the pan may have a designated front and back, or clips on the outer edge which need to engage in the machine to hold the bread pan in position. Fold the handle down and close the lid. Plug into the socket and switch on the power.

7 Select the programme you require, including crust colour and loaf size, if available. Press Start. The kneading process will begin, unless your machine has a "rest" period to settle the temperature first.

8 Towards the end of the kneading process the machine will beep to alert you to add any additional ingredients, such as dried fruit, if wished. Open the lid, add the extra ingredients, and close the lid again.

9 At the end of the cycle, the machine will beep once more to let you know that the dough is ready or the bread is cooked. Press Stop. Open the lid of the machine. If you are removing baked bread, remember to use oven gloves to lift out the bread pan, as it will be extremely hot. Avoid leaning over and looking into the machine when you open the lid as the hot air escaping from the machine could cause you discomfort.

BELOW: A basic white bread is an excellent choice for the novice bread maker. If you follow these instructions and weigh the ingredients carefully, you are sure to achieve a delicious loaf of bread. Once you have gained confidence, experiment with the recipe, by adding other ingredients or changing the crust colour.

10 Still using oven gloves, turn the pan upside down and shake it several times to release the bread. If necessary, tap the base of the pan on a heatproof board.

11 If the kneading blade for your bread machine is not of the fixed type, and comes out inside the bread, use a heat-resistant utensil to remove it, such as a wooden spatula. It will come out easily.

12 Place the bread on a wire rack to cool. Unplug the bread machine and leave to cool before using it again. A machine which is too hot will not make a successful loaf, and many will not operate if they are too hot for this reason. Refer to the manufacturer's manual for guidance. Wash the pan and kneading blade and wipe down the machine. All parts of the machine must be cool and dry before you store it.

BASIC CONTROLS

It will take you a little while and some practice to become familiar with and confident about using your new bread machine. Most manufacturers now produce excellent manuals, which are supplied with their machines. The manual is a good place to start, and should also be able to help you if you come up against a problem. Programmes obviously differ slightly from machine to machine, but an overview will give you a general idea of what is involved.

It is important to understand the function of each control on your bread machine before starting to make a loaf of bread. Each feature may vary slightly between different machines, but they all work in a basically similar manner.

START AND STOP BUTTONS

The Start button initiates the whole process. Press it after you have placed all the ingredients required for the bread-making procedure in the bread pan and after you have selected all the required settings, such as loaf type, size, crust colour and delay timer.

The Stop button may actually be the same control or a separate one. Press it to stop the programme, either during the programme, if you need to override it, or at the end to turn off the machine. This cancels the "keep warm" cycle at the end of baking.

TIME DISPLAY AND STATUS INDICATOR

A window displays the time remaining until the end of the programme selected. In some machines the selected programme is also shown. Some models use this same window or a separate set of lights to indicate what is happening inside the machine. It gives information on whether the machine is on time delay, kneading, resting, rising, baking or warming.

PROGRAMME INDICATORS OR MENU

Each bread machine has a number of programmes for different types of bread. Some models have more than others. This function allows you to choose the appropriate programme for your recipe and indicates which one you have selected. These programmes are discussed in more detail later.

PRE-HEAT CYCLE

Some machines start all programmes with a warming phase, either prior to mixing or during the kneading phase. This feature can prove useful on colder days or when you are using larger quantities of ingredients, such as milk, straight from the refrigerator, as you do not have to wait for them to come to room temperature before making the bread.

DELAY TIMER

This button allows you to pre-set the bread machine to switch on automatically at a specified time. So, for example, you can have freshly baked bread for breakfast or when you return from work. The timer should not be used for dough that contains perishable ingredients such as fresh dairy products or meats, which deteriorate in a warm environment.

CRUST COLOUR CONTROL

The majority of bread machines have a default medium crust setting. If, however, you prefer a paler crust or the appearance of a high-bake loaf, most machines will give you the option of a lighter or darker crust. Breads high in sugar, or that contain eggs or cheese, may colour too much on a medium setting, so a lighter option may be preferable for these.

WARMING INDICATOR

When the bread has finished baking, it is best to remove it from the machine immediately. If for any reason this is not possible, the warming facility will switch on as soon as the bread is baked, to help prevent condensation of the steam, which otherwise would result in a soggy loaf. Most machines continue in this mode for an hour, some giving an audible reminder every few minutes to remove the bread.

LEFT: French Bread can be baked in the machine on a French bread setting, or the dough can be removed to make the traditional shape by hand.

REMINDER LIGHTS

A few models are fitted with a set of lights which change colour after being activated, to serve as your reminder that certain essential steps have been followed. This helps to ensure that the kneading blade is fitted, and that basic ingredients such as liquid, flour and yeast have been placed in the bread pan.

LOAF SIZE

On larger bread machines you may have the option of making up to three different sizes of loaf. The actual sizes vary between individual machines, but approximate to small, medium and large loaves of around 450g/1lb, 675g/1½lb and 900g/2lb respectively. However, this control in some machines is for visual indication only and does not alter the baking time or cycle. Check the manufacturer's instructions.

BAKING PROGRAMMES

All machines have a selection of programmes to help ensure you produce the perfect loaf of bread. The lengths of kneading, rising and baking times are varied to suit the different flours and to determine the texture of the finished loaf.

BASIC OR NORMAL

This mode is the most commonly used programme, ideal for white loaves and mixed grain loaves where strong white (bread) flour is the main ingredient.

RAPID

This cycle reduces the time to make a standard loaf of bread by about 1 hour and is handy when speed is the main criterion. The finished loaf may not rise as much as one made on the basic programme and may therefore be a little more dense.

WHOLE WHEAT

This is a longer cycle than to allow time for the slower rising action of doughs containing a high percentage of strong wholemeal (whole-wheat) flour. Some machines also have a multigrain mode for breads made with cereals and grains such

ABOVE: Sun-dried tomatoes can be added to the dough at the raisin beep to make deliciously flavoured bread.

as Granary (multi-grain) and rye, although it is possible to make satisfactory breads using this or the basic mode, depending on the percentages of the flours.

FRENCH

This programme is best suited for low-fat and low-sugar breads, and it produces loaves with an open texture and crisper crust. More time within the cycle is devoted to rising, and in some bread machines the loaf is baked at a slightly higher temperature.

SWEET BREAD

A few bread machines offer this feature in addition to crust colour control. It is useful if you intend to bake breads with a high fat or sugar content which tend to colour too much.

CAKE

Again, this is a feature offered on a few machines. Some will mix a quick non-yeast teabread-type cake and then bake it; others will mix yeast-raised cakes. If you do not have this facility, teabreads and non-yeast cakes can easily be mixed in a bowl and cooked in the bread pan on a "bake only" cycle.

BAKE

This setting allows you to use the bread machine as an oven, either to bake cakes and ready-prepared dough from the supermarket or to extend the standard baking time if you prefer your bread to be particularly well done.

SANDWICH

This facility, which enables you to bake a loaf with a soft crust that is particularly suitable for sandwich slices, is available on one or two models only.

RAISIN BEEP

Additional ingredients can be added mid-cycle on most programmes. The machine gives an audible signal – usually a beep – and some machines pause late in the kneading phase so that ingredients such as fruit and nuts can be added. This late addition reduces the risk of them being crushed during the kneading phase.

If your machine does not have this facility, you can set a kitchen timer to ring 5 minutes before the end of the kneading cycle and add the extra ingredients then.

DOUGH PROGRAMMES

Most machines include a dough programme: some models have dough programmes with extra features.

DOUGH

This programme allows you to make dough without machine-baking it, which is essential for all hand-shaped breads. The machine mixes, kneads and proves the dough, ready for shaping, final rising and baking in a conventional oven. If you wish to make different shaped loaves or rolls, buns and pastries, you will find this facility invaluable.

OTHER DOUGH PROGRAMMES

Some machines include cycles for making different types of dough, such as a rapid dough mode for pizzas and focaccia or a longer mode for wholemeal dough and bagel dough. Some "dough only" cycles also include the raisin beep facility.

BAKING, COOLING AND STORING

A bread machine should always bake a perfect loaf of bread, but it is important to remember that it is just a machine and cannot think for itself. It is essential that you measure the ingredients carefully and add them to the bread pan in the order specified by the manufacturer of your machine. Ingredients should be at room temperature, so take them out of the refrigerator in good time, unless your machine has a pre-heat cycle.

Check the dough during the kneading cycles; if your machine does not have a window, open the lid and look into the bread pan. The dough should be slightly tacky to the touch. If it is very soft, add a little more flour; if the dough feels very firm and dry add a little more liquid. It is also worth checking the dough towards the end of the rising period. On particularly warm days your bread may rise too high. If this happens it may rise over the bread pan and begin to travel down the outside during the first few minutes of baking. If your bread looks ready for baking before the baking cycle is due to begin, you have two options. You can either override and cancel the programme, then re-programme using a "bake only" cycle, or you can try pricking the top of the loaf with a cocktail stick (toothpick) to deflate it slightly and let the programme continue.

Different machines will give different browning levels using the same recipe. Check when you try a new recipe and make a note to select a lighter or darker setting next time if necessary.

BELOW: Use a cocktail stick (toothpick) to prick dough that has risen too high.

REMOVING THE BREAD FROM THE PAN
Once the bread is baked it is best removed from the bread pan immediately. Turn the bread pan upside down, holding it with oven gloves or a thick protective cloth – it will be very hot – and shake it several times to release the bread. If removing the bread is difficult, rap the corner of the bread pan on a wooden board several times or try turning the base of the shaft underneath the base of the bread pan. Don't try to free the bread by using a knife or similar metal object, or you will scratch the non-stick coating.

If the kneading blade remains inside the loaf, you should use a heat-resistant plastic or wooden implement to prise it out. The metal blade and the bread will be too hot to use your fingers.

ABOVE: This bread is sweetened with honey which, like other sweeteners such as sugar, acts as a preservative. The loaf should stay moist for longer.

BELOW: Use a serrated bread knife when slicing bread so that you do not damage the texture of the crumb.

COOLING

Place the bread on a wire rack to allow the steam to escape and leave it for at least 30 minutes before slicing. Always slice bread using a serrated knife to avoid damaging the crumb structure.

STORING

Cool the bread, then wrap it in foil or place it in a plastic bag and seal it, to preserve the freshness. If your bread has a crisp crust, this will soften on storage, so until it is sliced it is best left uncovered. After cutting, put the loaf in a large paper bag, but try to use it fairly quickly, as bread starts to dry out as soon as it is cut. Breads containing eggs tend to dry out even more quickly, while those made with honey or added fats stay moist for longer.

BELOW: Parker House Rolls can be frozen after baking, as soon as they are cool. They taste delicious warm, so refresh them in the oven just before serving.

ABOVE: If you are freezing bread to be used for toasting, slice the loaf first.

Ideally, freshly baked bread should be consumed within 2–3 days. Avoid storing bread in the refrigerator as this causes it to go stale more quickly.

Freeze cooked breads if you need to keep them for longer. Place the loaf or rolls in a freezer bag, seal and freeze for up to 3 months. If you intend to use the bread for toast or sandwiches, it is easier

ABOVE: Store bread with a crispy crust in a large paper bag.

to slice it before freezing, so you can remove only the number of slices you need. Thaw the bread at room temperature, still in its freezer bag.

With some loaves, however, freezing may not be a sensible option. For example, very crusty bread, such as French Bread, tends to come apart after it has been frozen and thawed.

STORING BREAD DOUGHS

If it is not convenient to bake bread dough immediately, you can store it in an oiled bowl which has been covered with clear film (plastic wrap), or seal it in a plastic bag. Dough can be stored in the refrigerator for up to 2 days if it contains butter, milk or eggs and up to 4 days if it does not.

Keep an eye on the dough and knock it back (punch it down) occasionally. When you are ready, return it to room temperature, then shape, leave to rise and bake it in the normal way.

You can make dough in your machine, shape it, then keep it in the refrigerator overnight, ready for baking conventionally next morning for breakfast. Cover with oiled clear film as usual.

Bread dough can be frozen in a freezerproof bag for up to 1 month. When you are ready to use it, thaw the dough overnight in the refrigerator or at room temperature for 2–3 hours. Once it has thawed, place it in a warm place to rise, but bear in mind that it will take longer to rise than freshly made dough.

ABOVE: Store dough in the fridge in an oiled bowl covered in clear film (plastic wrap) or in a plastic bag.

ABOVE: Prepare rolls the night before and store in the refrigerator, ready to bake the following morning.

HAND-SHAPED LOAVES

One of the most useful features a bread machine can have is the dough setting. Use this, and the machine will automatically mix the ingredients, and will then knead and rest the dough before providing the ideal conditions for it to rise for the first time. The whole cycle, from mixing through to rising, takes around 1¾ hours, but remember it will vary slightly between machines.

KNOCKING BACK (PUNCHING DOWN)

1 At the end of the cycle, the dough will have almost doubled in bulk and will be ready for shaping. Remove the bread pan from the machine.

2 Lightly flour a work surface. Gently remove the dough from the bread pan and place it on the floured surface. Knock back or deflate the dough to relieve the tension in the gluten and expel some of the carbon dioxide.

3 Knead the dough lightly for about 1–2 minutes; shape into a ball. Some recipes suggest you cover it with oiled clear film (plastic wrap) or an upturned bowl and leave it to rest for a few minutes. This allows the gluten to relax so the dough will be easier to handle.

SHAPING

Techniques to shape dough vary, depending on the finished form of the bread you wish to make. The following steps illustrate how to form basic bread, roll and yeast pastry shapes.

BAGUETTE

1 To shape a baguette or French stick, flatten the dough into a rectangle about 2.5cm/1in thick, either using the palms of your hands or a rolling pin.

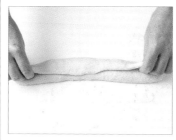

2 From one long side fold one-third of the dough down and then fold over the remaining third of dough and press gently to secure. Repeat twice more, resting the dough in between folds to avoid tearing.

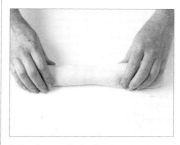

3 Gently stretch the dough and roll it backwards and forwards with your hands to make a breadstick of even thickness and the required length.

4 Place the baguette dough between a folded floured dish towel, or in a banneton, and leave in a warm place to prove. The dish towel or banneton will help the baguette to keep the correct shape as it rises.

BLOOMER

1 Roll the dough out to a rectangle 2.5cm/1in thick. Roll up from one long side and place it, seam side up, on a floured baking sheet. Cover and leave to rest for 15 minutes.

2 Turn the loaf over and place on another floured baking sheet. Using your fingertips, tuck the sides and ends of the dough under. Cover; leave to finish rising.

TIN LOAF

Roll the dough out to a rectangle the length of the bread tin (pan) and three times as wide. Fold it widthways, bringing the top third down and the bottom third up. Press the dough down well, turn it over and place it in the tin.

COTTAGE LOAF

1 To shape a cottage loaf, divide the dough into two pieces, approximately one-third and two-thirds in size. Shape each piece of dough into a plump round ball and place on lightly floured baking sheets. Cover with inverted bowls and leave to rise for 30 minutes, or until 50 per cent larger.

2 Flatten the top of the large loaf. Using a sharp knife, cut a cross about 4cm/1½in across in the centre. Brush the area lightly with water and place the small round on top.

3 Using one or two fingers or the floured handle of a wooden spoon, press the centre of the top round, penetrating into the middle of the dough beneath.

TWIST

1 To shape bread for a twist, divide the dough into two equal pieces. Using the palms of your hands, roll each piece of dough on a lightly floured surface into a long rope, about 4–5cm/1½–2in thick. Make both ropes the same length.

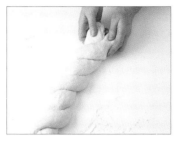

2 Place the two ropes side by side. Starting from the centre, twist one rope over the other. Continue in the same way until you reach the end, then pinch the ends together and tuck the join underneath. Turn the dough around and repeat the process with the other end, twisting the dough in the same direction as the first.

BREADSTICK

To shape a breadstick, roll the dough to a rectangle about 1cm/½in thick, and cut out strips that are about 7.5cm/3in long and 2cm/¾in wide. Using the palm of your hand, gently roll each strip into a long thin rope.

It may help to lift each rope and pull it very gently to stretch it. If you are still finding it difficult to stretch the dough, leave it to rest for a few minutes and then try again.

COURONNE

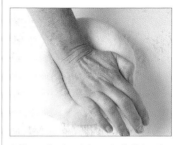

1 Shape the dough into a ball. Using the heal of your hand make a hole in the centre. Gradually enlarge the centre, turning the dough to make a circle, with a 13cm–15cm/5–6in cavity.

2 Place on a lightly oiled baking sheet. Put a small, lightly oiled bowl in the centre of the ring to prevent the dough from filling in the centre during rising.

SCROLL

Roll out the dough using the palms of your hands to form a rope, about 25cm/10in long, with tapered ends. Form into a loose "S" shape, then curl the ends in to make a scroll. Leave a small space to allow for the final proving (rising).

CROISSANT

1 To shape a croissant, roll out the dough on a lightly floured surface and then cut it into strips that are about 15cm/6in wide.

2 Cut each strip along its length into triangles with 15cm/6in bases and 18cm/7in sides.

3 Place with the pointed end towards you and the 15cm/6in base at the top; gently pull each corner of the base to stretch it slightly.

4 Roll up the dough with one hand from the base while pulling, finishing with the dough point underneath. Finally, curve the corners around in the direction of the pointed end to make the curved croissant shape.

PLAITED (BRAIDED) ROLL

1 To shape a plaited roll, place the dough on a lightly floured surface and roll out. Divide the dough into balls, the number depending on the amount of dough and how many rolls you would like to make.

2 Divide each ball of dough into three equal pieces. Using your hands, roll into long, thin ropes of equal length and place them side by side.

3 Pinch one of the ends together and plait (braid) the pieces of dough. Finally, pinch the remaining ends together and then tuck the join under.

FILLED PLAITED BRAID

1 Place the dough for the plaited braid on a lightly floured surface. Roll out and shape into a rectangle. Using a sharp knife, make diagonal cuts down each of the long sides of the dough, about 2cm/¾in wide. Place the filling in the centre of the uncut strip.

2 Fold in the end strip of dough, then fold over alternate strips of dough to form a plait over the filling. Tuck in the final end to seal the braid.

LEAVING TO RISE

After the dough has been shaped, it will need to be left to rise again. This is sometimes referred to as proving the dough. Most doughs are left in a warm place until they just about double in bulk. How long this takes will vary – depending on the ambient temperature and richness of the dough – but somewhere between 30 and 60 minutes is usual.

Avoid leaving dough to rise for too long (over-proving) or it may collapse in the oven or when it is slashed before baking. Equally, you need to leave it to rise sufficiently, or the finished loaf will be heavy.

To test if the dough is ready to bake, press it lightly with your fingertip; it should feel springy, not firm. The indentation made by your finger should slowly fill and spring back.

ABOVE: A dough that has been shaped and placed in a bread tin (pan) to rise. The unproved dough should reach just over halfway up the sides.

ABOVE: Leave the dough in a warm, draught-free place to rise. This should take between 30 and 60 minutes. Once risen, the dough will have almost doubled in bulk.

SLASHING

Slashing bread dough before baking serves a useful purpose as well as adding a decorative finish, as found on the tops of traditional loaf shapes such as bloomers and French sticks.When the dough goes into the oven it has one final rise, known as "oven spring", so the cuts or slashes allow the bread to expand without tearing or cracking the sides.

The earlier you slash the dough the wider the splits will be. Depth is important, too: the deeper the slashes the more the bread will open during baking. Most recipes suggest slashing just before glazing and baking. If you think a bread has slightly over-proved (over-risen) keep the slashes fairly shallow and gentle to avoid the possibility of the dough collapsing.

Use a sharp knife or scalpel blade to make a clean cut. Move smoothly and swiftly to avoid tearing the dough. Scissors can also be used to make an easy decorative finish to rolls or breads.

SLASHING A SPLIT TIN OR FARMHOUSE LOAF

A long slash, about 1cm/½in deep, can be made along the top of the dough just before baking. You can use this slashing procedure for both machine and hand-shaped loaves. Using a very sharp knife, plunge into one end of the dough and pull the blade smoothly along the entire length, but make sure you do not drag the dough.

If flouring the top of the loaf, sprinkle with flour before slashing.

SLASHING A BAGUETTE

To slash a baguette, cut long slashes of equal length and depth four or five times along its length. A razor-sharp blade is the best tool for slashing breads. Used with care, a scalpel is perfectly safe and has the advantage that the blades can be changed to ensure you always have a sharp edge.

USING SCISSORS TO SLASH ROLLS

Rolls can be given quick and interesting finishes using a pair of sharp-pointed scissors. You could experiment with all sorts of ideas. Try the following to start you off.
• Just before baking cut across the top of the dough first in one direction then the other to make a cross.
• Make six horizontal or vertical cuts equally spaced around the sides of the rolls. Leave for 5 minutes before baking.
• Cut through the rolls in four or five places from the edge almost to the centre, just before baking.

ABOVE: Top rolls: making a cross; middle rolls: horizontal cuts around the side; bottom rolls: cuts from the edge almost to the centre.

BAKING BREAD WITH A CRISP CRUST

For a crisper crust, it is necessary to introduce steam into the oven. The moisture initially softens the dough, so that it can rise, resulting in a crisper crust. Moisture also improves the crust colour by encouraging caramelization of the natural sugars in the dough. Standing the loaf on a baking stone or unglazed terracotta tiles also helps to produce a crisp crust, the effect being similar to when breads are cooked in a clay or brick oven. The porous tiles or stone hold heat and draw moisture from the bread base while it is baking.

1 About 30 minutes before you intend to bake, place the baking stone on the bottom shelf of the oven, then preheat the oven. Alternatively line the oven shelf with unglazed terracotta tiles, leaving air space all around to allow for the free circulation of the hot air.

2 When ready to bake, using a peel (baker's shovel), place the bread directly on the tiles or baking stone.

3 Using a water spray bottle, mist the oven walls two or three times during the first 5–10 minutes of baking. Open the oven door as little as possible, spray the oven walls and quickly close the door to avoid unnecessary heat loss. Remember not to spray the oven light, fan or heating elements.

GLAZES

B oth machine-baked breads and hand-shaped loaves benefit from a glaze to give that final finishing touch. Glazes may be used before baking, or during the early stages of baking to give a more golden crust or to change its texture of the crust. This is particularly noticeable with hand-shaped breads but good results may also be obtained with machine-baked loaves. Glazes may also be applied after baking to give flavour and a glossy finish. Another important role for glazes is to act as an adhesive, to help any topping applied to the loaf stick to the surface of the dough.

For machine-baked breads, the glaze should either be brushed on to the loaf just before the baking cycle commences, or within 10 minutes of the start of the baking cycle. Apply the glaze quickly, so there is minimal heat loss while the bread machine lid is open. Avoid brushing the edges of the loaf with a sticky glaze as this might make the bread stick to the pan.

Glazes using egg, milk and salted water can also be brushed over freshly cooked loaves. Brush the glaze over as soon as the baking cycle finishes, then leave the bread inside the machine for 3–4 minutes, to allow the glaze to dry to a shine. Then remove the loaf from the machine and pan in the usual way. This method is useful if you want to sprinkle over a topping.

For hand-shaped loaves, you can brush with glaze before or after baking, and some recipes, such as Parker House Rolls, will suggest that you do both.

GLAZES USED BEFORE OR DURING BAKING

For a crust with an attractive glossy shine, apply a glaze before or during baking.

MILK

Brush on loaves, such as potato breads, where a softer golden crust is desired. Milk is also used for bridge rolls, buns (such as teacakes) and flatbreads where a soft crust is desirable. It can also be used on baps and soft morning rolls before dusting with flour.

OLIVE OIL

Olive oil is mainly used to brush on Mediterranean-style breads, such as focaccia and Stromboli. It adds flavour and a shiny finish; and the darker the oil the fuller the flavour, so use extra virgin olive oil for a really deep taste. Olive oil can be used before and/or after baking.

BELOW: French fougasse is brushed with olive oil just before baking.

BUTTER

Rolls and buns are brushed with melted butter before baking to add colour, while also keeping the dough soft. Parker House Rolls are brushed before and after baking, while Coconut Milk Sugar Buns are brushed with melted butter and sprinkled with sugar. Butter adds a rich flavour to the breads glazed with it.

SALTED WATER

Mix 10ml/2 tsp salt with 30ml/2 tbsp water and brush over the dough immediately before baking. This gives a crisp baked crust with a slight sheen.

EGG WHITE

Use 1 egg white mixed with 15ml/1 tbsp water for a lighter golden, slightly shiny crust. This is often a better alternative to egg yolk for savoury breads.

EGG YOLK

Mix 1 egg yolk with 15ml/1 tbsp milk or water. This classic glaze, also known as egg wash, is used to give a very golden, shiny crust. For sweet buns, breads and yeast cakes add 15ml/1 tbsp sugar, for extra colour and flavour.

GLAZES ADDED AFTER BAKING

Some glazes are used after baking, often on sweet breads, cakes and pastries. These glazes generally give a glossy and/or sticky finish, and also help to keep the bread or cake moist. They are suited to both machine and hand-shaped breads.

BUTTER

Breads such as Italian Panettone and stollen are brushed with melted butter after baking to soften the crust. Clarified butter is also sometimes used as a glaze to soften flatbreads.

HONEY, MALT, MOLASSES AND GOLDEN (LIGHT CORN) SYRUP

Liquid sweeteners can be warmed and brushed over breads, rolls, teabreads and cakes to give a soft, sweet, sticky crust. Honey is a traditional glaze and provides a lovely flavour, for example. Both malt and molasses have quite a strong flavour, so use these sparingly, matching them to compatible breads such as fruit loaves and cakes. Or you could mix them with a milder-flavoured liquid sweetener, such as golden syrup, to reduce their impact slightly.

SUGAR GLAZE

Dissolve 30–45ml/2–3 tbsp granulated sugar in the same amount of milk or water. Bring to the boil, then simmer for 1–2 minutes, until syrupy. Brush over fruit loaves or buns for a glossy sheen. For extra flavour, use rose water.

SYRUPS

Yeast cakes are often drizzled with sugar syrup, flavoured with liqueurs, spirits or lemon juice. The syrup moistens the bread, while adding a decorative and flavoursome topping at the same time.

PRESERVES

Jam or marmalade can be melted with a little liquid. Choose water, liqueur, spirits (such as rum or brandy) or fruit juice, depending on the bread to be glazed. The liquid thins the preserve and adds flavour. It can be brushed over freshly baked warm teabreads, Danish Pastries and sweet breads to a give a glossy, sticky finish. Dried fruit and nuts can then be sprinkled on top.

Select a flavoured jam to complement your bread or teacake. If in doubt, use apricot jam.

ICING (CONFECTIONERS') SUGAR GLAZE

Mix 30–45ml/2–3 tbsp icing sugar with 15ml/1 tbsp fruit juice, milk, single (light) cream (flavoured with vanilla essence/extract) or water and drizzle or brush over warm sweet breads and cakes. You can also add a pinch of spice to the icing sugar to bring out the flavour of the loaf. Maple syrup can be mixed with the sugar for glazing nut-flavoured breads.

LEFT: The glossy top to Hot Cross Buns is achieved by glazing after baking with a mixture of milk and sugar.

TOPPINGS

In addition to glazes, extra ingredients can be sprinkled over breads to give the finished loaf further interest. Toppings can alter the appearance, flavour and texture of the bread, so are an important part of any recipe. They also allow you to add your own individual stamp to a bread by using a topping of your own invention.

MACHINE-BAKED BREADS

A topping can be added at various stages: at the beginning of the baking cycle, about 10 minutes after baking begins, or immediately after baking while the bread is still hot. If you choose to add the topping at the beginning of baking, open the lid only for the shortest possible time, so heat loss is limited to the minimum. Before you add a topping, brush the bread with a glaze. This will ensure that the topping sticks to the loaf. Most machine breads are brushed with an egg, milk or water glaze.

If applying a topping to a bread after baking, remove the bread pan carefully from the machine and close the lid to retain the heat. Using oven gloves, quickly loosen the bread from the pan, then put it back in the pan again (this will make the

ABOVE: *Flaked (sliced) almonds have been sprinkled over the top of this Raspberry and Almond Teabread, giving a broad hint of its delicious flavour and adding extra crunch.*

final removal easier) then brush the loaf with the glaze and sprinkle over the chosen topping. Return the bread in the pan to the bread machine for 3–4 minutes, which allows the glaze to bake on and secure the topping. With this method, the chosen topping will not cook and brown in the same way it would were it added at the beginning of baking.

When using grain as a topping, the general rule is to match it to the grain or flour used in the bread itself; for example, a bread containing millet flakes or millet seeds is often sprinkled with millet flour.

If a flavouring has been incorporated into the dough, you may be able to top the loaf with the same ingredient, to provide a hint of what is inside. Try sprinkling a little grated Parmesan on to a cheese loaf about 10 minutes after baking begins, or, for a loaf flavoured with herbs, add an appropriate dried herb as a topping immediately after baking.

LEFT: *Rolled oats and wheat grain are sprinkled on to Sweet Potato Bread just before it begins to bake to give the loaf a delightful rustic look.*

FLOUR

To create a farmhouse-style finish, brush the loaf with water or milk glaze just before baking – or within 10 minutes of the start of baking – and dust lightly with flour. Use white flour, or wholemeal (whole-wheat) for a more rustic finish.

SMALL SEEDS

Seeds can be used to add flavour and texture in addition to a decorative finish. Try sesame, poppy, aniseed, caraway or cumin seeds. If adding sesame seeds immediately after baking, lightly toast until golden before adding.

SALT

Brush the top of a white loaf with water or egg glaze and sprinkle with a coarse sea salt, to give an attractive and crunchy topping. Sea salt is best applied at the beginning of baking or 10 minutes into the baking cycle.

MAIZEMEAL (CORNMEAL) OR POLENTA

Use maizemeal, polenta, semolina or other speciality flours as a finish for breads containing these flours, brushing first with a water or milk glaze.

LARGE SEEDS

Gently press pumpkin or sunflower seeds on to the top of a freshly glazed loaf to give an attractive finish and a bonus crunch.

WHEAT AND OAT BRAN FLAKES

These add both texture and fibre to bread as well as visual appeal. Sprinkle them over the top of the loaf after glazing at the beginning of baking.

ROLLED OATS

These make a decorative finish for white breads and breads flavoured with oatmeal. Rolled oats are best added just before or at the very beginning of baking.

PEPPER AND PAPRIKA

Freshly ground black pepper and paprika both add spiciness to savoury breads. This tasty topping can be added before, during or after baking.

ICING (CONFECTIONERS') SUGAR

Dust cooked sweet breads, teabreads or cakes with icing sugar after baking for a finished look. If wished, add 2.5ml/½tsp spice before sprinkling for added flavour.

HAND-SHAPED BREAD

All of the toppings used on machine-baked breads can also be added to breads that are hand-shaped and baked in an oven. There are several methods that can be used for adding a topping to hand-shaped rolls and breads.

SPRINKLING WITH FLOUR

If you are using flour, this should be sprinkled over the dough immediately after shaping and again before slashing and baking, to give a rustic finish. Match the flour to the type of bread being made. Unbleached strong white (bread) flour is ideal for giving soft rolls and breads a fine finish. Use maizemeal (cornmeal), ground rice or rice flour for muffins and brown and wholemeal (whole-wheat) on wholegrain breads.

GROUND RICE OR RICE FLOUR

Muffins are enhanced with a ground rice or rice flour topping.

WHOLEMEAL (WHOLE-WHEAT) FLOUR

Wholemeal flour toppings complement wholegrain dough whether made into loaves or rolls.

ABOVE: An Easter Tea Ring is glazed with icing (confectioners') sugar and orange juice, then sprinkled with pecan nuts and candied orange.

ROLLING DOUGH IN SEEDS

Sprinkle seeds, salt or any other fine topping on a work surface, then roll the shaped but unproved dough in the chosen topping until it is evenly coated. This is ideal for coating wholegrain breads with pumpkin seeds or wheat flakes. After rolling, place the dough on the sheet for its final rising.

SESAME SEEDS

Dough sticks can be rolled in small seeds for a delicious crunchy topping.

ADDING A TOPPING AFTER A GLAZE

Some toppings are sprinkled over the bread after glazing and immediately before baking. In addition to the toppings suggested for machine-baked breads, these toppings can be used:

CANDIED FRUITS

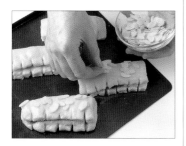

Whole or chopped candied fruits make an attractive topping for festive breads. Add the fruits after an egg glaze. They can also be used after baking, with a jam or icing (confectioners') sugar glaze to stick the fruits to the bread.

NUTS

Just before baking, brush sweet or savoury breads and rolls with glaze and sprinkle with chopped or flaked (sliced) almonds, chopped cashews, chopped or whole walnuts or pecan nuts.

> **SMALL SEEDS AND GRAINS**
>
> Seeds and grains, such as millet grain, black onion seeds and mustard seeds, all add texture and taste to breads. Try them as a topping for loaves and flatbreads.

VEGETABLES

Brush savoury breads and rolls with an egg glaze or olive oil and then sprinkle with finely chopped raw onion, raw (bell) peppers, sun-dried tomatoes or olives for an extremely tasty crust.

CHEESE

Grated cheeses, such as Parmesan, Cheddar or Pecorino, are best for sprinkling on to dough just before baking, resulting in a chewy, flavoursome crust.

FRESH HERBS

Use fresh herbs, such as rosemary, thyme, sage or basil for Italian-style flatbreads. Chopped herbs also make a good topping for rolls.

USING SUGAR AS A TOPPING

Sugar is available in many forms, so chose one appropriate for your topping.

DEMERARA (RAW) SUGAR

Before baking, brush buns and cakes with butter or milk, then sprinkle with demerara sugar for a crunchy finish.

SUGAR COATING

Yeast doughs that are deep-fried, such as Doughnuts, can be sprinkled or tossed in a sugar coating. Toss doughnuts in caster (superfine) sugar that has been mixed with a little ground cinnamon or freshly grated nutmeg, or flavoured using a vanilla pod (bean).

ICING (CONFECTIONERS') SUGAR

Use a fine sieve to sprinkle cooked buns and yeast cakes, such as Devonshire Splits and Calas, with a light dusting of icing sugar. Large cakes and breads, such as Panettone, also benefit from a light dusting of icing sugar. If you are serving a bread or cake warm, dust with icing sugar when ready to serve to prevent the topping from soaking into the bread.

Getting the Best from Your Machine

Even the most comprehensive bread-machine manual cannot possibly cover all the hints and tips you will need. As you gain experience and confidence you will be able to solve more and more of any little problems that crop up. Here are a few pointers to help you along the road to successful baking.

Temperature and Humidity

The bread machine is not a sealed environment, and temperature and humidity can affect the finished results. On dry days, dry ingredients contain less water and on humid days they hold more.

The temperature of the ingredients is a very important factor in determining the success of machine-baked bread. Some machines specify that all ingredients should be at room temperature; others state that ingredients can be added from the refrigerator. Some machines have pre-heating cycles to bring the ingredients to an optimum temperature of around 20–25°C/68–77°F, before mixing starts. It is recommended that you use ingredients at room temperature. Water can be used straight from the cold tap. Lukewarm water may be beneficial for the rapid bake cycle on cold days.

Hot weather can mean that doughs will rise faster, so on very hot days start with chilled ingredients, using milk or eggs straight from the refrigerator.

Icy winter weather and cold draughts will inhibit the action of the yeast, so either move your machine to a warmer spot, or warm liquids before adding them to the bread pan. On very cold days, let the water stand at room temperature for about half an hour before adding the other ingredients to the pan, or add a little warm water to bring it up to a temperature of around 20°C/68°F, but no hotter.

Quality Produce

Use only really fresh, good quality ingredients. The bread machine cannot improve poor quality produce. Make sure the yeast is within its use-by date. Yeast beyond its expiry date will produce poor results.

Measuring Ingredients

Measure both the liquids and the dry ingredients carefully. Most problems occur when ingredients are inaccurately measured, when one ingredient is forgotten or when the same ingredient is added twice. Do not mix imperial and metric measurements, as they are not interchangeable; stick to one set for the whole recipe.

Do not exceed the quantities of flour and liquid recommended for your machine. Mixing the extra ingredients may overload the motor and if you have too much dough it is likely to rise over the top of the pan.

Follow the Instructions

Always add the ingredients in the order suggested by the manufacturer. Whatever the order, keep the yeast dry and separate from any liquids added to the bread pan.

Adding Ingredients

Cut butter into pieces, especially if it is fairly firm, and/or when larger amounts than usual are required in the recipe. If a recipe requires ingredients such as cooked vegetables or fruit or toasted nuts to be added, leave them to cool to room temperature before adding them.

Using the Delay Timer

Perishable ingredients such as eggs, fresh milk, cheese, meat, fruit and vegetables may deteriorate, especially in warm conditions, and could present a health risk. They should only be used in breads that are made immediately. Only use the delay timer for bread doughs that contain non-perishable ingredients.

CLEANING YOUR MACHINE

Unplug the machine before starting to clean it. Wipe down the outside regularly using a mild washing-up liquid (dishwashing detergent) and a damp, soft cloth. Avoid abrasive cleansers and materials, even those designated for use on non-stick items, and alcohol-based cleansers.

Bread Pan and Kneading Blade

Clean the bread pan and blade after each use. These parts should not be washed in the dishwasher as this might affect the non-stick surface and damage the packing around the shaft. Avoid immersing the bread pan in water. If you have difficulty extracting the blade from the pan, fill the base of the pan with lukewarm water and leave it to soak for a few minutes. Remove the blade and wipe it with a damp cloth. Wash the bread pan with mild washing-up liquid then rinse thoroughly. Always store the bread machine with the kneading blade removed from the shaft. The bread machine and components must be completely dry before putting away.

*ABOVE: A Granary (multi-grain) loaf
should be baked on the whole-wheat
setting, with its longer rising cycle.*

SPECIAL CONSIDERATIONS

Breads made with whole grains and
heavier flours such as wholemeal (whole-wheat), oatmeal or rye, or with added
ingredients such as dried fruits and nuts,
are likely to rise more slowly than basic
white loaves. The same applies to breads
with a lot of fat or egg. Breads that include
cheese, eggs or a high proportion of fats
and/or sugar are more susceptible to burning. To avoid over-cooked crusts, select a
light bake crust setting.

WATCHING THE DOUGH

Keep a flexible rubber spatula next to the
machine and, if necessary, scrape down
the sides of the pan after 5–10 minutes of
the initial mixing cycle. The kneading
blade sometimes fails to pick up a thick or
sticky dough from the corners of the pan.

COOLING THE BREAD

It is best to remove the loaf from the pan
as soon as the baking cycle finishes, or it
may become slightly damp, even with a
"stay warm" programme.

CHECKING THE DOUGH

Check the dough within the first 5 minutes of mixing, especially when you are
trying a recipe for the first time. If the
dough seems too wet and, instead of forming a ball, sticks to the sides of the pan,
add a little flour, a spoonful at a time.
However, the bread machine requires a
dough that is slightly wetter than if you
were mixing it by hand. If the dough is
crumbly and won't form a ball, add liquid,
one spoonful at a time. You will soon get
used to the sound of the motor and notice
if it is labouring due to a stiff mix. It is also
worth checking the dough just before baking, to make sure it isn't about to rise over
the top of the bread machine pan.

*ABOVE: Dough is too wet and requires
more flour.*

*ABOVE: Dough is too dry and requires
more water.*

SAFETY

1 Read the manufacturer's advice
and instructions before operating
your machine. Keep any instruction
manuals provided with your
machine handy for future reference.
2 If you touch the machine while it
is in operation, be careful. The
outside walls become hot when it is
in baking mode.
3 Position the machine on a firm,
level, heat-resistant surface, away
from any other heat source.
4 Do not stand the bread machine in
direct sunlight and allow at least
5–7.5cm/2–3in clearance on all sides
when not in use.
5 Do not place anything on top of
the machine lid.
6 Do not use the machine outdoors.
7 Do not immerse the machine,
cable or plug in water and avoid
using it near a source of water.
8 Be careful to keep your fingers
away from the blade while the
machine is kneading the dough, and
never reach inside the machine
during the baking cycle.
9 Keep the machine out of the
reach of small children and make
sure there is no trailing cable.
10 Unplug the machine before
cleaning or moving it, and when it is
not in use. Allow the bread machine
to cool completely before cleaning
and storing it.

ADAPTING RECIPES FOR USE IN A MACHINE

After you have cooked a number of the recipes from this book you may wish to branch out and adapt some of your own favourites. This sample recipe is used to explain some of the factors you will need to take into consideration.

INGREDIENTS

Read the list of ingredients carefully before you start, and adjust if necessary.

MALT EXTRACT AND GOLDEN (LIGHT CORN) SYRUP

High sugar levels may cause bread to over-brown. Reduce the malt extract and syrup quantities by one-third and increase other liquids to compensate. Machine breads require the inclusion of sugar. Allow 5–10ml/1–2 tsp per 225g/8oz/2 cups flour.

BUTTER

High fat levels mean that the bread will take longer to rise. Reduce to 50g/2oz/¼ cup per 450g/1lb/4 cups flour. You may need to add an extra 30ml/2 tbsp liquid.

FLOUR

This recipe uses white flour, but remember that a wholemeal (whole-wheat) loaf works better if you replace half the wholemeal flour with strong white (bread) flour.

YEAST

Replace fresh yeast with easy-blend (rapid-rise) dried yeast. In a wholemeal bread, for example, start by using 5ml/1 tsp for up to 375g/13oz/3¼ cups flour or 7.5ml/1½ tsp for up to 675g/1½lb/6 cups.

MILK

Use skimmed milk at room temperature where possible. If you wish to use the time delay cycle you should replace fresh milk with milk powder.

DRIED FRUIT

Additions that enrich the dough, such as dried fruits, nuts, seeds and wholegrains, make the dough heavier, and the bread will not rise as well. Limit them to about a quarter of the total flour quantity.

MALTED FRUIT LOAF

50g/2oz/scant ¼ cup malt extract
30ml/2 tbsp golden (light corn) syrup
75g/3oz/6 tbsp butter
450g/1lb/4 cups unbleached strong white (bread) flour
5ml/1 tsp mixed (apple pie) spice
20g/¾oz fresh yeast
150ml/5fl oz/⅔ cup lukewarm milk
50g/2oz/¼ cup currants
50g/2oz/⅓ cup sultanas (golden raisins)
50g/2oz/¼ cup ready-to-eat dried apricots
25g/1oz/2 tbsp mixed chopped (candied) peel

FOR THE GLAZE
30ml/2 tbsp milk
30ml/2 tbsp caster (superfine) sugar

MAKES 2 LOAVES

1 Grease two 450g/1lb loaf tins (pans).
2 Melt the malt extract, syrup and butter in a pan. Leave to cool.
3 Sift the flour and spice into a large bowl; make a central well. Cream the yeast with a little of the milk; blend in the rest. Add the yeast mixture with the malt extract to the flour and make a dough.
4 Knead on a floured surface until smooth and elastic, about 10 minutes. Place in an oiled bowl; cover with oiled clear film (plastic wrap). Leave to rise in a warm place for 1½–2 hours.
5 Turn the dough out on to a lightly floured surface and knock back (punch down). Gently knead in the dried fruits.
6 Divide the dough in half; shape into two loaves. Place in the tins and cover with oiled clear film. Leave to rise for 1–1½ hours or until the dough reaches the top of the tins.
7 Preheat the oven to 200°C/400°F/ Gas 6. Bake the loaves for 35–40 minutes, or until golden. Transfer to a wire rack.
8 Gently heat the milk and sugar for the glaze. Brush over the warm loaves.

METHOD

Use a similar bread machine recipe as a guide for adapting a conventional recipe.

STEP 1

Obviously, you can only make one machine-baked loaf at a time. Make 1 large loaf or reduce the quantity of ingredients if your machine is small.

STEP 2

There is no need to melt the ingredients before you add them, but remember to chop the butter into fairly small pieces.

STEP 3

When adding ingredients to the bread pan, pour in the liquid first, then sprinkle over the flour, followed by the mixed spice. (Add the liquid first unless your machine requires dry ingredients to be placed in the bread pan first.)

Add easy-blend dried yeast to a small indent in the flour, but make sure it does not touch the liquid underneath.

Place salt and butter in separate corners of the pan. If your recipe calls for egg, add this with the water or other liquid.

Use water straight from the tap and other liquids at room temperature.

STEPS 4–7

Ignore these steps, apart from adding the fruit. The bread machine will automatically mix, rise and cook the dough. Use a light setting for the crust due to the sugar, fat and fruit content of the Malted Fruit Loaf. Ordinary breads, such as a white loaf, need a medium setting; loaves that contain wholemeal flour should be baked on the whole wheat setting.

If you are adding extra ingredients, such as dried fruit, set the bread machine on raisin setting and add the ingredients when it beeps. If you do not have this facility, add approximately 5 minutes before the end of the kneading cycle.

STEP 8

Make the glaze as usual and brush over the loaf at the end of the baking cycle.

USEFUL GUIDELINES

Here are a few guidelines that are worth following when adapting your own favourite recipes.

• Make sure the quantities will work in your machine. If you have a small bread machine, it may be necessary to reduce them. Use the flour and water quantities in recipes in the book as a guide, or refer back to your manufacturer's handbook.

• It is important that you keep the flour and the liquid in the correct proportions, even if reducing the quantities means that you end up with some odd amounts. You can be more flexible with spices and flavourings such as fruit and nuts, as exact quantities are not so crucial.

• Monitor the recipe closely the first time you make it and jot down any ideas you have for improvements next time.

• Check the consistency of the dough when the machine starts mixing. You may need to add one or two extra spoonfuls of water, as breads baked in a machine

BELOW: Use a similar bread machine recipe to help you adapt a bread you usually make conventionally. So, if you have a favourite swede (rutabaga) bread recipe, try adapting a machine recipe for parsnip bread.

ABOVE: Some conventional recipes call for you to knead ingredients, such as fried onions, into a dough. When adapting for a bread machine, add to the dough at the raisin beep.

require a slightly softer dough, which is wet enough to relax back into the shape of the bread pan.

• If a dough mixes perfectly in your machine but then fails to bake properly, or if you want bread of a special shape, use the dough cycle on your machine, then shape by hand before baking in a conventional oven.

• Look through bread machine recipes and locate something that is similar. This will give you some idea as to quantities, and which programme you should use. Be prepared to make more adjustments after testing your recipe for the first time.

USING BREAD MIXES

Packaged bread mixes can be used in your machine. Check your handbook, as some manufacturers may recommend specific brands.

• Check that your machine can handle the amount of dough the bread mix makes. If the packet quantity is only marginally more than you usually make, use the dough cycle and then bake conventionally.

• Select an appropriate setting; for instance, use the normal or rapid setting for white bread.

1 Place the recommended amount of water in the bread pan.

2 Spoon over the bread mix and place the pan in the machine.

3 Select the programme required and press Start. Check the consistency of the dough after 5 minutes, adding a little more water if the mixture seems too dry.

4 At the end of the baking cycle, remove the cooked bread from the bread pan and turn out on to a wire rack to cool.

TROUBLESHOOTING

Bread machines are incredibly easy to use and, once you have become familiar with yours, you will wonder how you ever did without it. However, they are machines and they cannot think for themselves. Things can go wrong and you need to understand why. Here are a few handy troubleshooting tips.

BREAD RISES TOO MUCH

• Usually caused by too much yeast; reduce by 25 per cent.
• An excess of sugar will promote yeast action; try reducing the quantity of sugar.
• Did you leave out the salt or use less than was recommended? If so, the yeast would have been uncontrolled and a tall loaf would have been the likely result.
• Too much liquid can sometimes cause a loaf to over-rise. Try reducing by 15–30ml/1–2 tbsp next time.
• Other possibilities are too much dough or too hot a day.

BREAD DOES NOT RISE ENOUGH

• Insufficient yeast or yeast that is past its expiry date.
• A rapid cycle was chosen, giving the bread less time to rise.

• The yeast and salt came into contact with each other before mixing. Make sure they are placed in separate areas when added to the bread pan.
• Too much salt inhibits the action of the yeast. You may have added salt twice, or added other salty ingredients, such as ready-salted nuts or feta cheese.
• Wholegrain and wholemeal (whole-wheat) breads tend not to rise as high as white flour breads. They contain bran and wheat germ, making the flour heavier.
• You may have used a plain (all-purpose) white flour instead of a strong (bread) flour, which has a higher gluten content.
• The ingredients were not at the correct temperature. If they were too hot, they may have killed the yeast; if they were too cold, they may have retarded the action of the yeast.
• Insufficient liquid. In order for dough to rise adequately, it needs to be soft and pliable. If the dough was dry and stiff, add more liquid next time.
• The lid was open during the rising stage for long enough to let warm air escape.
• No sugar was added. Yeast works better where there is at least 5ml/1 tsp sugar to feed it. Note, however, that high sugar levels may retard yeast action.

BREAD DOES NOT RISE AT ALL

• No yeast was added or it was past its expiry date.
• The yeast was not handled correctly and was probably killed by adding ingredients that were too hot.

THE DOUGH IS CRUMBLY AND DOESN'T FORM A BALL

• The dough is too dry. Add extra liquid a small amount at a time until the ingredients combine to form a pliable dough.

THE DOUGH IS VERY STICKY AND DOESN'T FORM A BALL

• The dough is too wet. Try adding a little extra flour, a spoonful at a time, waiting for it to be absorbed before adding more. You must do this while the machine is still mixing and kneading the dough.

BREAD MIXED BUT NOT BAKED

• A dough cycle was selected. Remove the dough, shape it and bake it in a conventional oven or bake it in the machine on the "bake only" cycle.

BREAD COLLAPSED AFTER RISING OR DURING BAKING

• Too much liquid was added. Reduce the amount by 15–30ml/1–2 tbsp next time, or add a little extra flour.
• The bread rose too much. Reduce the amount of yeast slightly in the future, or use a quicker cycle.
• Insufficient salt. Salt helps to prevent the dough from over-proving (over-rising).
• The machine may have been placed in a draught or may have been knocked or jolted during rising.
• High humidity and warm weather may have caused the dough to rise too fast.
• Too much yeast may have been added.
• The dough may have contained a high proportion of cheese.

THERE ARE DEPOSITS OF FLOUR ON THE SIDES OF THE LOAF

• The dry ingredients, especially the flour, stuck to the sides of the pan during kneading, and then adhered to the rising dough. Next time, use a flexible rubber spatula to scrape down the sides of the pan after 5–10 minutes of the initial mixing cycle, if necessary, but take care to avoid the kneading blade.

CRUST IS SHRIVELLED OR WRINKLED

• Moisture condensed on top of the loaf while it was cooling. Remove from the bread machine as soon as it is cooled.

CRUMBLY, COARSE TEXTURE

• The bread rose too much; try reducing the quantity of yeast slightly next time.
• The dough didn't have enough liquid.
• Too many whole grains were added. These soaked up the liquid. Next time, either soak the whole grains in water first or increase the general liquid content.

BURNT CRUST

• There was too much sugar in the dough. Use less or try a light crust setting for sweet breads.
• Choose the sweet bread setting if the machine has this option.

PALE LOAF

• Add milk, either dried or fresh, to the dough. This encourages browning.
• Set the crust colour to dark.
• Increase the sugar slightly.

CRUST TOO CHEWY AND TOUGH

• Increase the butter or oil and milk.

BREAD NOT BAKED IN THE CENTRE OR ON TOP

• Too much liquid was added; next time, reduce the liquid by 15ml/1 tbsp or add a little extra flour.
• The quantities were too large and your machine could not cope with the dough.
• The dough was too rich; it contained too much fat, sugar, eggs, nuts or grains.
• The bread machine lid was not closed properly, or the machine was used in too cold a location.
• The flour may have been too heavy. This can occur when you use rye, bran and wholemeal (whole-wheat) flours. Replace some of it with strong white (bread) flour.

CRUST TOO SOFT OR CRISP

• For a softer crust, increase the fat and use milk instead of water. For a crisper crust, do the opposite.
• Use the French bread setting for a crisper crust.
• Keep a crisper crust by lifting the bread out of the pan and turn it out on to a wire rack as soon as the baking cycle finishes.

AIR BUBBLE UNDER THE CRUST

• The dough was not mixed well or didn't deflate properly during the knock (punch) down cycle between risings. This is likely to be a one-off problem, but if it persists, try adding an extra spoonful of water.

ADDED INGREDIENTS WERE CHOPPED UP INSTEAD OF REMAINING WHOLE

• They were added too soon and were chopped by the kneading blade. Add on the machine's audible signal, or 5 minutes before the end of the kneading cycle.
• Leave chopped nuts and dried fruits in larger pieces.

ADDED INGREDIENTS NOT MIXED IN

• They were probably added too late in the kneading cycle. Next time, add them a couple of minutes sooner.

THE BREAD IS DRY

• The bread was left uncovered to cool too long and dried out
• Breads low in fat dry out rapidly. Increase the fat or oil in the recipe.
• The bread was stored in the refrigerator. Next time place in a plastic bag when cool and store in a bread bin.

BREAD HAS A HOLEY TEXTURE

• The dough was too wet; use less liquid.
• Salt was omitted.
• Warm weather and/or high humidity caused the dough to rise too quickly.

A STICKY LAYERED UNRISEN MESS

• You forgot to put the kneading blade in the pan before adding the ingredients.
• The kneading blade was not correctly inserted on the shaft.
• The bread pan was incorrectly fitted.

SMOKE EMITTED FROM THE MACHINE

• Ingredients were spilt on the heating element. Remove the bread pan before adding ingredients, and add any extra ingredients carefully.

OTHER FACTORS

Creating the ideal conditions for your bread machine is largely a matter of trial and error. Take into account the time of year, the humidity and your altitude. Bread machines vary between models and manufacturers, and flour and yeast may produce slightly different results from brand to brand or country to country. Breads made in Australia, for example, often need slightly more water than those made in Britain.

You will soon get to know your machine. Watch the dough as it is mixing and check again before it begins to bake. Make a note of any tendencies (do you generally need to add more flour? does the bread often over-rise?) and adapt recipes accordingly.

FLOUR

The largest single ingredient used in bread, the right flour is the key to good bread making. Wheat is the primary grain for grinding into flour. Apart from rye, wheat is the only flour with sufficient gluten to make a well-leavened bread.

WHEAT FLOURS

Wheat consists of an outer husk or bran that encloses the wheat kernel. The kernel contains the wheat germ and the endosperm, which is full of starch and protein. It is these proteins that form gluten when flour is mixed with water. When dough is kneaded, gluten stretches like elastic to trap the bubbles of carbon dioxide, the gas released by the action of the yeast, and the dough rises.

Wheat is defined as either soft or hard, depending on its protein content, and is milled in various ways to give the wide range of flours we know today.

Wheat is processed to create many sorts of flour. White flours, for example, contain about 75 per cent of the wheat kernel. The outer bran and the wheat germ are removed to leave the endosperm, which is milled into a white flour. Unbleached flour is the best type to use, as it has not been chemically treated to make it unnaturally white. This type is gradually replacing much of the bleached flour.

RIGHT: Clockwise from top: strong, French, self-raising and plain flour

ABOVE: Clockwise from top left: Granary, stoneground strong wholemeal, strong brown, stoneground wholemeal

PLAIN (ALL-PURPOSE) WHITE FLOUR

A multi-purpose flour, plain white flour contains less protein and gluten than strong (bread) flour, typically around 9.5–10 per cent. Sometimes a small amount of this type of flour is mixed with strong flour to achieve a closer-grained texture, but the main use for plain white flour is in quick teabreads, when chemical raising agents such as baking powder are added to give a light, airy crumb.

STRONG WHITE (BREAD) FLOUR

This flour is milled from hard wheat flour, which has a higher protein level than soft wheat flour. Levels vary between millers but the typical figure is around 12 per cent. Some types of strong (bread) flour have lower levels – around 10.5–11 per cent – but these have ascorbic acid added to act as a dough enhancer.

SELF-RAISING (SELF-RISING) FLOUR

This is not used in traditional breads, but is ideal for quick teabreads and cakes cooked in the bread machine. Sodium bicarbonate (baking soda) and calcium phosphate are mixed into the flour and act as raising agents.

FINE FRENCH PLAIN (ALL-PURPOSE) FLOUR

Used in France for baking, this unbleached light flour is very fine and thus free-flowing. A small amount is often added to French bread recipes to reduce the gluten content and achieve the texture associated with baguettes and other specialities.

ORGANIC FLOURS

Organic white flour is produced using only natural fertilizers, and the wheat has not been sprayed with pesticides. Organic strong (bread) flours can be used in any recipe, and are recommended when developing natural yeasts for starters and sourdoughs.

WHOLEMEAL (WHOLE-WHEAT) FLOURS

Made from the complete kernel, including the bran and wheat germ, wholemeal is coarse textured and full-flavoured with a nutty taste. For making machine breads, you should use strong wholemeal (whole-wheat bread) flour, with a protein content of around 12.5 per cent. Plain wholemeal flour can be used with baking powder or bicarbonate of soda (baking soda) for teabreads. Loaves made with 100 per cent strong wholemeal flour tend to be very dense. The bran inhibits the release of gluten, so the dough rises more slowly. For these reasons, many machine recipes recommend blending strong wholemeal flour with some strong white flour.

Stoneground flour results when complete wheat grain is ground between two stones. Other wholemeal flours have the bran and wheat germ removed during milling and replaced afterwards.

STRONG BROWN (BREAD) FLOUR

This flour contains about 80–90 per cent of the wheat kernel, with some of the bran removed. A good alternative to wholemeal (whole-wheat) flour, it produces a loaf with a lighter finish, but with a denser texture and fuller flavour than white bread.

GRANARY (MULTI-GRAIN) FLOUR

A combination of wholemeal (whole-wheat), white and rye flours mixed with malted wheat grains, this adds texture and a contributes a flavour that is slightly sweet and nutty. Malthouse is similar.

ABOVE: Left to right: semolina, spelt

SPELT FLOUR

Rich in nutrients, this is made from spelt grain, an ancient precursor of modern wheat. It is best used in combination with strong white flour. Even though it contains gluten, some gluten-intolerant people can digest it, so it is included in some diets for people who are allergic to wheat.

SEMOLINA

A high gluten flour, semolina is made from the endosperm of durum or hard winter wheat before it is fully milled into a fine flour. It can be ground to a coarse granular texture or a finer flour. The finer flour is traditionally used for making pasta, but also makes a delicious bread when combined with other flours. If 100 per cent semolina is used, a heavy loaf will result.

OTHER WHEAT GRAINS

WHEAT BRAN

This is the outer husk of the wheat, which is separated from white flour during processing. It adds fibre, texture and flavour. You can add a spoonful to your favourite recipe or use it in place of part of the strong white (bread) flour.

WHEAT GERM

The germ is the embryo or heart of the wheat grain kernel. Use in its natural state, or lightly toasted, giving a nutty flavour. Wheat germ is a rich source of vitamin E and increases the nutritional value of bread. However, it inhibits the action of gluten, so do not use more than 30ml/2 tbsp for every 225g/8oz/2 cups flour.

CRACKED WHEAT

This is whole wheat kernel, broken into rather large pieces. It is quite hard, so you may like to soften it. Simmer in hot water for 15 minutes, then drain and cool. Add 15–30ml/1–2 tbsp to a dough 5 minutes before the end of the kneading cycle.

BELOW: Clockwise from top left: bran, bulgur wheat, wheat germ, cracked wheat

BULGUR WHEAT

This is made from the wheat grain. It is partially processed by boiling, which cracks the wheat kernel. Add to bread doughs, to give a crunchy texture. There is no need to cook it first. However you may wish to soak it in water first, to soften it further.

NON-WHEAT FLOURS

RYE FLOUR

Rye flour is used extensively in breads, partly because it grows well in climates that are cold and wet and not suitable for wheat cultivation. This is why so many of the Russian and Scandinavian breads include rye. Light and medium rye flours are produced from the endosperm, while dark rye includes all the grain, resulting in a coarser flour which adds more texture to the bread. Rye contains gluten, but when used on its own produces a very heavy bread. Rye dough is sticky and difficult to handle. For machine-made breads, rye flour must be combined with other flours. Even a small amount adds a distinctive tang.

MILLET FLOUR

Another high-protein, low-gluten grain, millet produces a light yellow flour with a distinctly sweet flavour and a slightly gritty texture. It tends to give breads a dry, crumbly texture, so you may need to add extra fat when using it. If using millet flour, boost the gluten content of the dough by using at least 75 per cent strong white (bread) flour.

BARLEY

Barley seeds are processed to remove the bran, leaving a product called pearl barley. This is ground to make barley flour, which is mild, slightly sweet and earthy. It gives breads a soft, almost cake-like texture, as it has a very low gluten content. White flour must be combined with barley flour in a ratio of at least 3:1 for machine bread.

BUCKWHEAT FLOUR

This greyish-brown flour has a distinctive, bitter, earthy flavour. Buckwheat is the seed of a plant related to the rhubarb family. It is rich in calcium and vitamins A and B, high in protein but low in gluten. Traditionally used to make pancakes, Russian blinis and French galettes, it is best used in combination with other flours, to produce full-bodied and tasty multigrain breads.

BELOW: Top to bottom: millet, buckwheat, barley

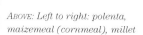

ABOVE: Left to right: polenta, maizemeal (cornmeal), millet

OTHER GRAINS

OATMEAL

When oats are cleaned and the outer husk has been removed, what remains is the oat kernel or groat. This is then cut into pieces to make either fine, medium or coarse oatmeal, or fully ground to make flour. All of these ingredients can be used in multigrain breads, adding a rich flavour and texture. The coarser the oats, the more texture they will contribute to the

ABOVE: Top to bottom: oatmeal, rye

bread. Oatmeal contains no gluten, so it needs to be combined with wheat flour for bread making. The coarser textured oatmeal makes an attractive topping on breads and rolls.

POLENTA AND MAIZEMEAL (CORNMEAL)

Dried corn kernels are ground to make coarse, medium and fine meal. The medium grain is known as polenta and the fine grain as maizemeal or cornmeal. For bread making, this gluten-free flour has to be combined with strong white (bread) flour. It adds a sweet flavour and an attractive yellow colour to the dough. For shaping the bread by hand, use polenta, which is slightly coarser and adds a pleasant finish to the bread.

MILLET GRAIN

This tiny, golden yellow, round grain is used in breads in Europe and Russia to give added texture. Include 15–30ml/ 1–2 tbsp in a multigrain bread, or even in a simple basic white loaf, for added interest. Millet grains make an attractive topping for breads. Millet flakes are also used in some breads.

RICE

Rice grains can be used in a variety of ways. Cooked long grain rice can be added to doughs for bread with a moist crumb. Wild rice, although strictly an aquatic grass, will add a beautiful texture and flavour. Add it near the end of the kneading cycle to keep the grain intact and give attractive dark flecks of colour to the bread. Ground rice and rice flour are milled from rice grains. Both brown and white rice flour are used, brown flour being more nutritious. Ground rice is more granular, similar to semolina. Either can replace some strong white (bread) flour in a recipe; they will

ABOVE: Clockwise from top left: ground rice, rice flour, wild rice, long grain rice

add a sweet flavour and chewy texture to the bread. Ground rice and rice flour can also be used as toppings. They are often dusted over English muffins or crumpets.

As rice is gluten-free, use only a small percentage of it with the strong flour, otherwise your loaf of bread will be rather dense.

ROLLED OATS

The inedible husk is removed from the oat kernel and the grain is then sliced, steamed and rolled to produce rolled oats. You can get jumbo-size oat flakes as well as traditional old-fashioned rolled oats.

For bread making, use the old-fashioned oats rather than the "quick cook" oats. Add rolled oats to bread doughs to give a chewy texture and nutty taste, or use as a topping for an attractive finish on rolls and breads.

OAT BRAN

High in soluble fibre, this is the outer casing of the oat kernel. It acts in a similar way to wheat bran, reducing the elasticity of the gluten, so use a maximum of 15ml/1 tbsp per 115g/4oz/1 cup flour. When using oat bran, you may need to add a little extra liquid to the dough.

LEFT: Clockwise from top right: jumbo oats, rolled oats, oat bran

LEAVENS AND SALT

Yeast is a living organism which, when activated by contact with liquid, converts the added sugar or sucrose, and then the natural sugars in the flour, into gases. These gases cause the bread to rise. As yeast is live, you must treat it with respect. It works best within the temperature range 21–36°C/70–97°F. Too hot and it will die; too cold and it will not activate. Yeast must be used before its use-by date, as old yeast loses its potency and eventually dies.

In most bread machine recipes dried yeast is used. In this book, all the recipes have been tested using easy-blend (rapid-rise) dried yeast, which does not need to be dissolved in liquid first. It is also called fast-action yeast. If you can find dried yeast especially made for use in bread machines, this will produce good results. You may need to adjust the quantities in individual recipes as variations occur between different makes of yeast.

ABOVE: Place dried yeast in a shallow indent in the flour.

ABOVE: Fresh yeast is dissolved before placing in the bread pan.

ABOVE: Yeast is available in two forms, fresh and dried. From top to bottom: fresh yeast, dried yeast.

ABOVE: Add liquid to dissolve and activate fresh yeast.

Fresh yeast is considered by some bakers to have a superior flavour. It can be used with caution when baking in a bread machine, but is best used in the "dough only" cycle. It is hard to give exact quantities for breads, which will be made using a range of machines operating in different temperatures. The difficulty lies in preventing the bread from rising over the top of the bread pan during baking; doughs made from easy-blend dried yeast are easier to control where uniform results are required.

NATURAL LEAVENS

Long before yeast was sold commercially, sourdough starters were used to make breads. These were natural leavens made by fermenting yeast spores that occurred naturally in flour, dairy products, plant matter and spices. Breads are still produced by the same method today. Breads made using natural leavens have different flavours and textures from the breads made with commercial yeast.

BELOW: Buckwheat and Walnut Bread is made using easy-blend (rapid-rise) dried yeast, which gives good results.

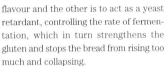

CHEMICAL LEAVENS

Raising agents other than yeasts can be used for bread. When using a bread machine, these are best used for teabreads and cakes that are mixed in a bowl, then baked in the bread pan.

Bicarbonate of soda (baking soda) is an alkaline raising agent that is often used for quick breads. When moistened with liquid it gives off carbon dioxide, which makes the cake or quick bread rise. The heat from the oven cooks and sets the risen batter before it can collapse.

Cream of tartar is an acid, which is often combined with bicarbonate of soda to boost the latter's leavening qualities. It also helps to neutralize the slightly soapy taste from the bicarbonate of soda.

BELOW: Bicarbonate of soda is the raising agent used for this Apricot, Prune and Peach Teabread

Baking powder is a ready-made mixture of acid and alkaline chemicals, usually bicarbonate of soda and cream of tartar, but sometimes bicarbonate of soda and sodium pyrophosphate. All these raising agents are fast acting. The bubbles are released the moment the powder comes into contact with a liquid, so such breads must be mixed and baked quickly.

SALT

Bread without salt tastes very "flat". While it is possible to make a saltless bread (there is, in fact, a famous saltless Tuscan bread which is eaten with salty cheese or preserved meats such as salami), salt is normally an indispensable ingredient. Salt has two roles: one is to improve the flavour and the other is to act as a yeast retardant, controlling the rate of fermentation, which in turn strengthens the gluten and stops the bread from rising too much and collapsing.

When adding salt to the bread pan, it is vital to keep it away from the yeast, as concentrated salt will severely impede the activity of the yeast.

Fine table salt and sea salt can both be used in bread that is to be baked in a machine. Coarse sea salt is best used as a topping. It can be sprinkled on top of unbaked breads and rolls to give a crunchy texture and agreeable flavour.

Salt substitutes are best avoided as few of these contain sodium.

DOUGH CONDITIONERS

These are added to breads to help stabilize the gluten strands and hold the gases formed by the yeast. Chemical conditioners are often added to commercially-produced bread, and you will also find bread improvers listed among the ingredients on fast-action yeast packets.

Two natural dough conditioners which help to ensure a higher rise, lighter texture, and stronger dough are lemon juice and malt extract. Gluten strength can vary between bags of flour, and lemon juice will help strengthen the bread dough, particularly when making wholegrain breads. You can add 5ml/1 tsp lemon juice with every 225g/8oz/2 cups strong (bread) flour without affecting the flavour of the bread.

Malt extract helps to break down the starch in wheat into sugars for the yeast to feed on and so encourages active fermentation. If you use up to 5ml/1 tsp malt extract with every 225g/8oz/2 cups strong flour you will not effect a noticeable flavour change. If you like the flavour of malt extract, you can increase the amount used.

LIQUIDS

Some form of liquid is essential when making bread. It rehydrates and activates the yeast, and brings together the flour and any other dry ingredients to make the dough. Whatever the liquid, the temperature is important for successful machine breads. If your machine has a preheating cycle, cold liquids, straight from the refrigerator, can be used. If not, use liquids at room temperature, unless it is a very hot day. Water from the tap, providing it is merely cool, is fine. On a very cold day, measure the water and leave it to stand in the kitchen for a while so that it acclimatizes before you use it.

WATER

Water is the most frequently used liquid in bread making. Bread made with water has a crisper crust than when milk is included. Tap water is chemically treated, and if it has been heavily chlorinated and fluorinated this may well slow down the rising. Hard water can also affect the rise, because it is alkaline, which retards the yeast. If your breads are not rising very well and you have tried other remedies, then either boil some water and let it cool to room temperature or use bottled spring water.

BELOW: Cranberry juice and orange juice may be used in teabreads.

MILK

Milk helps to enrich the dough and produces a creamy-coloured, tender crumb and golden crust. Use full-cream, semi-skimmed (low-fat) or skimmed milk, according to your preference. You can also replace fresh milk with skimmed milk powder (non fat dry milk). This can be useful if you intend using the timer to delay the starting time for making bread, as, unlike fresh milk, the milk powder will not deteriorate. Sprinkle it on top of the flour in the bread pan to keep it separated from the water until mixing starts.

BUTTERMILK

Used instead of regular milk, this makes bread more moist and gives it an almost cake-like texture. Buttermilk is made from skimmed milk which is pasteurized, then cooled. After this a cultured bacteria is added which ferments it under controlled conditions to produce its slightly tangy, acidic, but pleasant flavour. This flavour is noticeable in the finished loaf.

ABOVE: Clockwise from top left: milk, buttermilk, milk powder

Yogurt and Other Dairy Products

Another alternative to milk, yogurt also has good tenderizing properties. Use natural yogurt or try flavoured ones, such as lemon or hazelnut in similarly flavoured breads.

Sour cream, cottage cheese and soft cheeses such as ricotta, fromage frais and mascarpone can all be used as part of the liquid content of the bread. They are valued more for their tenderizing properties than for their flavour.

Coconut Milk

Use 50:50 with water to add flavour to sweet breads and buns.

Fruit Juices

Fruit juices such as orange, mango, pineapple or cranberry can be added to the dough for fruit-flavoured breads to enhance their fruitiness.

Vegetable Juices and Cooking Liquids

The liquid left over from cooking vegetables will add flavour and extra nutritional value to breads and is particularly useful when making savoury breads. Potato water has several benefits. The extra starch acts as an additional food for the yeast, and produces a greater rise and also a softer, longer-lasting loaf.

Vegetables themselves contain liquid juices and when added to a bread machine will alter the liquid balance.

Soaking Juices

When dried vegetables such as mushrooms, especially wild ones, and sun-dried tomatoes are rehydrated in water, a

ABOVE: Ciders, beers and liqueurs all add a rich, interesting flavour to breads.

flavoursome liquid is produced. This is much too good to waste. Rehydrate the vegetables, drain off the liquid and add it as part of the liquid in a savoury bread. In sweet breads, the liquid drained from dried fruits that have been plumped up in fruit juices, spirits and liqueurs is equally useful.

Beers, Ales, Ciders and Liqueurs

All of these can be added to bread recipes. Beers and ales, in particular, have a great affinity with dark, heavy flours. The added sugars stimulate the yeast by providing more food. Dark beers and ales impart a stronger flavour.

Eggs

If a bread recipe includes eggs, these should be considered part of the liquid content. Eggs add colour, improve the structure and give the bread a rich flavour, although it is inclined to dry out more quickly than plain bread. It is worth adding extra fat to compensate for this. All the recipes in this book use medium eggs unless stated otherwise.

ABOVE: Use soaking and cooking liquids in savoury breads.

FATS AND SWEETENERS

FATS

Whether solid (butter, margarine) or liquid (oil), small amounts of fats are often added to breads. They enrich doughs and add flavour, and, with eggs, they give a soft, tender texture to the crumb. Fats help to extend the freshness of the loaf, and in rich doughs, help to cancel out the drying effect that eggs can cause.

In small amounts, fat contributes to the elasticity of the gluten, but use too much and the opposite effect will result. The fat coats the gluten strands and this forms a barrier between the yeast and flour. This slows down the action of the yeast, and hence increases the rising time. For this reason it is best to limit the amount of fat in a machine-baked bread, or risk a heavy, compact loaf.

When making rich, brioche-style bread, it is best to use the bread machine only for making the dough. It may be necessary to use the cycle twice. Afterwards, shape the dough by hand and leave it to rise for as long as required, before baking the bread conventionally.

SOLID FATS

Butter, margarine or lard (shortening) can all be used in small quantities (of up to 15g/½oz/1 tbsp) without adding any noticeable flavour to the dough. Where a recipe calls for a larger quantity of fat, use butter, preferably unsalted (sweet). If you have only salted butter, and you are using quite a lot of it, you may need to reduce the amount of salt added to the dough. Cut the butter into small pieces so that it will mix in better. Avoid letting the fat come into contact with the yeast as it may inhibit the dissolving of the yeast.

BELOW: Left to right: olive oil, sunflower oil, hazelnut oil and walnut oil can all be used to impart a slightly different flavour to bread.

Where butter is layered in yeast pastry for croissants and Danish pastries, it is important to soften it so it has the same consistency as the dough. Although it is possible to use low-fat spreads in bread-making, there is not much point in doing so, as they may contain up to 40 per cent water and do not have the same properties as butter.

LIQUID FATS

Sunflower oil is a good alternative to butter if you are concerned about the cholesterol level, while olive oil can be used where flavour is important. Use a fruity, full-flavoured extra virgin olive oil from the first pressing of the olives.

Nut oils, such as walnut and hazelnut, are quite expensive and have very distinctive flavours, but are wonderful when teamed with similarly flavoured breads.

Fats and oils are interchangeable in many recipes. If you wish to change a solid fat for a liquid fat or oil the amount of liquid in the dough needs to be adjusted to accommodate the change. This is only necessary for amounts over 15ml/1 tbsp.

LEFT: Left to right: margarine, butter, lard (shortening)

ABOVE: Left to right:
dark brown sugar;
light brown muscovado (molasses)
sugar; light brown sugar; granulated
sugar; caster (superfine) sugar

SWEETENERS

Sugars and liquid sweeteners accelerate the fermentation process by providing the yeast with extra food. Modern types of yeast no longer need sugar; they are able to use the flour efficiently to provide food. Even so, it is usual to add a small amount of sweetener. This makes the dough more active than if it were left to feed slowly on the natural starches and sugars in the flour. Enriched breads and heavy whole-grain breads need the increased yeast action to help the heavier dough to rise.

Sugar helps delay the staling process in bread because it attracts moisture. It also creates a tender texture. Too much sugar can cause dough to over-rise and collapse. Sweet breads have a moderate sugar level and gain extra sweetness from dried fruits, sweet glazes and icings.

BELOW: Left to right: treacle, golden
syrup, molasses, malt extract,
maple syrup, honey

Sweeteners contribute to the colour of the bread. A small amount enhances the crust colour, giving a golden finish. Some bread machines over-brown sweet doughs, so select a light crust setting or a sweet bread setting, if available, when making sweet yeast cakes.

Any liquid sweetener can be used instead of sugar, but should be counted as part of the total liquid content of the bread. Adjustments may need to be made.

WHITE SUGARS

Granulated or caster (superfine) sugar can be used for bread making. They are almost pure sucrose and add little flavour. Do not use icing (confectioners') sugar as the anti-caking agent can affect the flavour. Save it for glazing and dusting.

BROWN SUGARS

Use light or dark brown, refined or unre-fined brown sugar. The darker unrefined sugars will add more flavour, having a higher molasses content. Brown sugars add a touch of colour and also increase the acidity, which can be beneficial.

MALT EXTRACT

An extract from malted wheat or barley, this has a strong flavour, so use sparingly. It is best used in fruit breads.

HONEY AND MAPLE SYRUP

Clear honey can be used as a substitute for sugar, but only use two-thirds of the amount suggested for sugar, as it is sweeter. Maple syrup is the reduced sap of the maple tree; use it in place of honey or sugar. It is slightly sweeter than sugar but not as sweet as honey.

MOLASSES, GOLDEN (LIGHT CORN) SYRUP AND TREACLE

All these sweeteners are by-products of sugar refining. Molasses is a thick con-centrated syrup with a sweet, slightly bitter flavour. It adds a golden colour to bread. Golden syrup is light and sweet with a slight butterscotch flavour. Treacle is brownish black and more intensely flavoured, and, like molasses, adds a slight bitterness to the bread.

ADDITIONAL INGREDIENTS

MEATS

Meats can be used to flavour bread recipes. The best results often come from using cured meats, such as ham, bacon or salami, and cooked sausages such as pepperoni.

When you use a strongly flavoured meat, it is best to chop it finely and add it to the dough during its final kneading. You don't need much – 25–50g/1–2oz will be quite sufficient to add extra flavour without overpowering the bread.

Ham and bacon are best added as small pieces, late on in the kneading cycle. Dice ham small. Fry or grill (broil) bacon rashers (strips), then crumble them or cut into pieces, or use ready-cut cubes of bacon or pancetta and sauté them first. Make sure the bacon is fully cooked before adding it to the bread dough.

LEFT: Sausages and bacon are a good addition to bread. They should be cooked before adding to a dough.

Thinly sliced preserved meats, such as prosciutto, pastrami, speck, pepperoni and smoked venison can be added as thin strips towards the end of the kneading cycle or incorporated in the dough during shaping, for hand-shaped loaves. Cured and smoked venison marinated in olive oil and herbs gives a basic loaf of bread a wonderful burst of flavour, or you could try adding pastrami to a bread containing rye flour.

Strongly flavoured meats will make the most impact, but remember that you need only small amounts.

USING BACON IN A BREAD MACHINE

1 Cut the bacon into thin strips and grill (broil) it, or dry-fry in a non-stick frying pan, until it is crisp.

2 Transfer the cooked bacon to a plate lined with kitchen paper, to blot up excess fat. Leave to cool.

3 Add the strips to the breadmaking machine towards the end of the kneading process or when the machine beeps.

USING MEATS

Some meats are best kept whole or coarsely chopped and used as a filling, as when sausage is layered through a brioche dough, or used as a topping on tray-baked breads and pizzas. There are many different types of salami, flavoured with spices such as peppercorns, coriander or paprika, as well as pepperoni and cooked spicy Continental-style sausages, all of which are suitable.

LEFT: From top to bottom: salami, pepperoni, thinly sliced smoked venison, prosciutto

RIGHT: From left to right: cream cheese, mascarpone, natural (plain) yogurt

CHEESES

Cheese can be added to a wide variety of breads, to make them more moist and to give them more taste. Some cheeses have powerful flavours that really impact on the bread, while others are much more subtle, and are indistinguishable from the other ingredients except for the richness and tenderness they impart. Yogurt and soft cheeses such as cottage cheese, ricotta and mascarpone are added in this way as part of the liquid content of the recipe. They contribute little to the over-all taste of the bread, but help to create a more tender loaf with a softer crumb.

Grated or chopped hard cheeses can be added at the beginning of kneading so they are totally incorporated in the dough, or else towards the end of kneading, meaning that small amounts can clearly be detected in the bread. Alternatively, the cheese can be sprinkled over the top just before baking, to add colour and tex-ture to the crust, or used as a topping or filling, as in pizzas or calzones.

For maximum cheese flavour, use small amounts of strongly flavoured cheeses such as Cheddar, Parmesan, Pecorino, or blue cheeses such as Roquefort, Gorgonzola, Danish Blue or Stilton.

If the cheese is salty, reduce the amount of added salt, or the action of the yeast will be retarded and the bread may taste unacceptably salty.

Machine-made breads incorporating hard cheeses may not rise as high as ones without, due to the increased richness in the dough, but the texture and flavour are likely to be superb.

RIGHT: Selection of cheeses, clockwise from top left: Cheddar, Emmenthal, feta, Gorgonzola; centre: mozzarella

HERBS AND SPICES

Use herbs and spices as the main flavouring ingredient in bread or to enhance other ingredients.

HERBS

Fresh herbs have the most wonderful aroma, matched only by their flavour in freshly baked breads. Use fresh herbs if possible. Dried herbs that are oily and pungent, such as sage, rosemary and thyme, also work well. Rosemary is especially pungent, so use sparingly. Dried oregano is a fine substitute for fresh. Dried herbs have a more concentrated flavour than fresh; use about a third of the quantity recommended for fresh.

A number of herbs are now available freshly chopped and preserved in oil, which is a good alternative for more delicate herbs such as basil and coriander

LEFT: Clockwise from top: basil, thyme, flat leaf parsley, oregano, coriander (cilantro), dill

BELOW: From left to right: Front row: black onion seeds, saffron, fennel, nutmeg; back row: allspice, cinnamon, cumin, ginger

(cilantro) which do not dry well. Add fresh herbs toward the end of the kneading cycle. Dried herbs can be added with the dry ingredients. Avoid dried parsley; substitute a different herb instead.

SPICES

Spices are the dried, intensely aromatic, seeds, pods, stems, bark, buds or roots of plants. As with herbs, the fresher they are the more aromatic they will be; the volatile oils fade with age. Use freshly grated black pepper and nutmeg. Cumin, fennel, caraway and cardamom can be bought as whole seeds, and ground in a spice mill, or a coffee mill kept for the purpose, as needed. If you buy ground spices, use them within 6 months.

Add saffron, nutmeg, cinnamon, anise, all-spice and cardamom to sweet or savoury breads. Mixed (apple pie) spice and ginger are sweet spices, while juniper berries, cumin, coriander and black onion seeds provide aromatic flavourings for savoury breads. A number of whole spices can also be used as toppings for breads.

ADDING HERBS AND SPICES

• Frozen chopped herbs are a quick alternative to fresh herbs. Add them to the dough just before the end of the kneading process.
• Add ground spices after the flour, so they do not come into contact with the liquid before mixing.
• Add whole spices along with the dry ingredients if you want them to break down during kneading. If not, add them when the machine beeps, towards the end of kneading.

NUTS

Nuts make a wonderful addition to home-made breads. Their crunchiness combines equally well with the sweet chewiness of dried and semi-dried fruits, and with fresh fruits. They go well with savoury additions such as cheese, herbs and spices and they can be used on their own to make rustic-style breads.

Nuts contain natural oils which turn rancid if stored too warm or for too long. Buy in small quantities, store in an air-tight container in a cool place and use them within a few weeks.

Pecan nuts, almonds, macadamia nuts, pistachio nuts and walnuts give wonderful flavour and texture when added to basic breads towards the end of the kneading process. They can be added to teabreads, or used as a decoration on top of sweet breads or yeast cakes. Walnut bread is a rich brown loaf with a soft crunch, perfect with cheeses.

Lightly toast pine nuts, hazelnuts and almonds first to bring out their flavour. Spread the nuts on a baking sheet and place them in an oven preheated to 180°C/350°F/Gas 4 for 5–8 minutes, or grill (broil) until golden. Avoid scorching, and cool before adding them to the bread.

Hazelnuts, almonds and walnuts can be finely ground and used as a nutritious and flavoursome flour substitute. Replace up to 15 per cent of the flour with the ground nuts. If using hazelnuts, remove the skin first, as it is bitter. This will easily rub off if you toast the nuts in the oven.

Use grated fresh or desiccated (dry, unsweetened shredded) coconut.

CHESTNUT BREAD

These quantities are for a medium loaf. Increase all ingredients by 25 per cent for a large machine; decrease by 25 per cent for a small one.

1 Combine 175g/6oz/½ cup chestnut purée with 250ml/9fl oz/scant 1¼ cups water. Place in the bread pan. Add the dry ingredients first if necessary.

2 Add 450g/1lb/4 cups strong white (bread) flour and 50g/2oz/½ cup wholemeal (whole-wheat) flour with 30ml/2 tbsp skimmed milk powder (non fat dry milk), 2.5ml/½tsp ground cloves and 5ml/1 tsp grated nutmeg. Place 5ml/1 tsp salt, 15ml/1 tbsp muscovado (molasses) sugar and 45ml/3 tbsp butter in the pan. Make an indent; add 7.5ml/1½tsp easy-blend dried (rapid-rise) yeast.

3 Set to the basic/normal setting, with raisin setting (if available), light crust. Press Start. Add 75g/3oz/¾ cup coarsely chopped walnuts at the beep or after the first kneading. Cool on a wire rack.

VEGETABLES

Raw, canned, dried and freshly cooked vegetables all make perfect additions to savoury breads. Making bread also provides a good opportunity to use up any leftover cooked vegetables. Vegetable breads are richer than basic breads, the vegetables contributing flavour and texture to the finished loaves. Many vegetable breads are subtly coloured or dotted with attractive flecks.

Fresh vegetables are relatively high in liquid, so if you add them, calculate that about half of their weight will be water

BELOW: Clockwise from top: spinach, green, red and yellow (bell) peppers, courgettes (zucchini), sweet potatoes

LEFT: Clockwise from top right: garlic, spring onions (scallions), chilli peppers, dried sliced onion, onions

and deduct the equivalent amount of liquid from the recipe. Keep an eye on the dough as it mixes and add more flour or liquid as needed.

STARCHY VEGETABLES

Potatoes, sweet potatoes, parsnips, carrots and other varieties of starchy vegetables sweeten the bread and contribute a soft texture. You can use leftover mashed or even instant potato, adding 115g/4oz/1½ cups–225g/8oz/2⅔ cups to a basic bread recipe depending on the size of your machine. Adjust the liquid accordingly.

SPINACH

Fresh spinach leaves need to be blanched briefly in boiling water before being used. After blanching, add them whole with the liquid ingredients at the beginning

(BELL) PEPPERS

1 Cut each pepper into three or four flat pieces, removing the seeds. Place in a grill (broiler) pan or roasting tin (pan) and brush the pieces lightly with olive oil or sunflower oil.

2 Grill (broil) until the skins blister and begin to char. Remove each piece as it is cooked and place inside a plastic bag. Seal the bag and leave to cool.

3 Peel off and discard the skin, then chop the peppers and add when the bread machine beeps, or 5 minutes before the kneading cycle ends.

LEFT: Fresh or dried mushrooms work well in breads

of the kneading process, and they will mix in and become finely chopped as the cycle progresses. Frozen chopped spinach can be substituted for fresh, but thaw it completely first and reduce the liquid in the recipe to allow for the extra water.

ONIONS, LEEKS AND CHILLIES
These vegetables are best if you sauté them first in a little butter or oil, which brings out their flavour. Caramelized onions will add richness and a light golden colour to the bread. For speed, you can add dried sliced onions instead of fresh onions, but you may need to add an extra 15ml/1 tbsp or so of liquid.

MUSHROOMS
Dried wild mushrooms can be used in the same way as sun-dried tomatoes to produce a very tasty loaf for serving with soups, casseroles and stews. Strain the soaking water, if you intend to use it in a recipe, to remove any grit.

TOMATOES
Tomatoes are very versatile and give bread a delicious flavour. They can be puréed, canned, fresh or sun-dried. Depending on when you add sun-dried tomatoes they will either remain as pieces, making a bread with interesting flecks of colour, or be fully integrated in the dough to provide flavour. To intensify the taste, choose regular sun-dried tomatoes, rather than the ones preserved in oil,

reconstitute them in water, then use the soaking water as the liquid in the recipe. Other tomato products are best added at the beginning of the breadmaking cycle, to ensure a richly coloured, full-bodied loaf with a distinct tomato flavour.

OTHER VEGETABLES
Add vegetables such as sweetcorn kernels, chopped olives or spring onions (scallions) towards the end of the kneading cycle to ensure that they remain whole. All will impart flavour, colour and texture.

Frozen vegetables should be thawed completely before using in the machine. You may need to reduce the liquid quantity in the recipe if you use frozen vegetables instead of fresh. Canned vegetables should be well drained.

CHICKPEAS
The starchiness of chickpeas, like that of potatoes, produces a light bread with good keeping qualities. Add cooked drained chickpeas whole; the machine will reduce them to a pulp very effectively. Chickpeas add a pleasant, nutty flavour to breads.

ADDING VEGETABLES TO BREAD
There are several ways of preparing vegetables ready to add to the machine.

• Add grated raw vegetables, such as beetroot (beet) or carrots, when you add the water to the bread pan.

• Sweet potatoes, parsnips, potatoes, winter squashes and pumpkin should be cooked first. Drain, reserving the cooking liquid, and mash them. When cool, add both the cooking liquid and the mashed vegetable to the dough.

• If you want vegetables to remain identifiable in the finished bread, add them when the machine beeps for adding extra ingredients or 5 minutes before the end of the kneading cycle, so they stay as slices or small pieces.

FRUIT

Whether you use them fresh, dried or as purées or juices, fruits add complementary flavours to breads and teacakes. The natural sugars help to feed the yeast and improve the leavening process, while fruits with natural pectin will improve the keeping quality of baked goods.

DRIED CAKE FRUITS

The familiar dried cake fruits such as sultanas (golden raisins), currants and raisins can easily be incorporated in basic breads, adding their own distinctive flavours. Sprinkle them in gradually, when the machine beeps or towards the end of the kneading cycle. For added flavour, plump them up in fruit juice or liqueur. You can add up to 50g/2oz/¼ cup of dried fruit for a small bread machine, 115g/4oz/⅔ cup

ABOVE: Pears, bananas, apples

for a large machine. If you soak the dried fruit first, use the excess as part of the measured liquid. You may need to add a spoonful or so of extra liquid to a basic bread recipe if you do not soak the fruit first.

BELOW: Clockwise from top left: candied citrus peel, dried pears, dried cranberries, prunes, dried mango, dried figs

RIGHT: Strawberries, raspberries, blueberries

DRIED, SEMI-DRIED AND READY-TO-EAT DRIED FRUITS

These are perfect for breads, because their flavours are so concentrated, and there is a vast range to choose from. Use combinations of exotic dried fruits, such as mango, papaya, melon and figs. Small dried fruits such as cranberries and cherries can be added whole, while the larger exotic fruits need to be chopped coarsely, as do apricots, pears, dates and peaches. Dried fruits such as prunes can be soaked in sherry or a liqueur, as for cake fruits.

FRESH FRUITS

Some fruits such as berries can be frozen before they are added to the dough. This helps to keep them intact. Spread the fruits out in a single layer on a baking sheet and freeze them until they are solid. Add to the dough in the machine just before the end of the kneading cycle. You can also use ready-frozen fruits in this way. When adding juicy fruits, toss them with a little extra flour, to keep the consistency of the bread dough correct. Soft fruits can be added to teabread mixtures too; just fold them in at the end of mixing.

Firm fruits, such as apples or pears, can be added raw, chopped into small chunks. Plums and rhubarb can also be used raw; simply cut them into small pieces. Rhubarb can also be poached first, so that it softens slightly. You can also grate firm fruits, or mash soft ripe fruits such as bananas and pears.

TROPICAL FRUIT BREAD

These quantities are for a medium loaf. Increase all ingredients by 25 per cent for a large machine; decrease by 25 per cent for a small one.

1 Pour 60ml/4 tbsp pineapple juice and 200ml/7fl oz/⅞ cup buttermilk into the pan. Mash 1 large banana (about 180g/6½oz) and add. Add the dry ingredients first if your machine specifies this.

2 Sprinkle over 450g/1lb/4 cups strong white (bread) flour and 50g/2oz/½ cup wholemeal (whole-wheat) flour. Place 5ml/1 tsp salt, 45ml/3 tbsp sugar and 40g/1½oz/3 tbsp butter in separate corners. Make an indent in the flour; add 5ml/1 tsp easy-blend (rapid-rise) dried yeast.

3 Set to the basic/normal setting, with raisin setting (if available), light crust. Press Start. Add 75g/3oz/½ cup chopped pineapple chunks at the beep or towards the end of the cycle. Remove from the pan and turn out on to a wire rack.

ADDING FRUIT TO BREADS

When you add the fruit and how heavily processed it is will determine whether it remains clearly detectable as whole pieces or blends fully into the dough to impart an even flavour and moistness throughout the bread.

• Add frozen orange concentrate or fruit juice right at the beginning of the mixing process, unless the instructions for your machine state you should add the dry ingredients first.

• Add purées, such as apple, pear or mango, after the water in the recipe has been poured into the bread pan. Alternatively, blend the two together first, then add the mixture to the pan.

BELOW: Fruit juice can replace part of the water quantity in some breads. Left to right: apple juice, pineapple juice, mango juice

• If you wish to add mashed or grated fruits, such as bananas or pears, put them in after the liquids.

• Add fresh or frozen whole fruits, such as berries, when the machine beeps or about 5 minutes before the end of the kneading cycle. Chopped fruits, such as apples and plums, as well as dried fruits, should also be added towards the end of the kneading process.

EQUIPMENT

The accessories required for bread-making are quite simple, the most expensive being the bread machine, which you probably already own. The essential pieces of equipment are largely concerned with accurate measuring; the remaining items are useful for hand-shaped breads.

MEASURING

Items to measure ingredients accurately are vital for making machine breads.

SCALES

Electronic scales give the most accurate results and are well worth investing in. You can place the bread pan directly on the scales and weigh the ingredients straight into it. The display can be set to zero after each ingredient has been added, which makes additions to the pan easy to perform and absolutely precise.

MEASURING SPOONS

Smaller quantities of dry ingredients, such as sugar, salt and, most importantly, yeast, need to be measured carefully. A set of measuring spoons from 1.5ml/¼ tsp to 15ml/1 tbsp is ideal. Always level off the ingredient in the spoon for an accurate measure.

MEASURING JUGS (CUPS)

Heatproof glass jugs that are clearly marked in metric and imperial units are very useful. Place the jug on a flat surface to ensure accuracy, and check the level of the ingredients by bending down so that the measurements are at eye level.

LEFT: Having a range of different-size glass bowls is useful.

LEFT: Bannetons may be used for final proving before the bread is baked.

LEFT: Use scales and measuring jugs, cups and spoons to ensure the correct quantity of ingredients. Accuracy is essential to give good results.

MIXING AND RISING

The bread machine will automatically mix dough and make it rise, but there may be some items of equipment you need for hand-shaped breads.

GLASS BOWLS

While most of the mixing will take place inside the machine, you will still need to mix glazes, add extra ingredients, transfer doughs or batters to a large bowl, or use a large bowl as a cover for hand-shaped bread during the final proving period. Glass bowls give all-round visibility and a selection of sizes will prove universally useful around the kitchen.

BELOW: A French baguette tray will give French loaves their traditional shape.

LEFT: Speciality cake tins (pans) such as a kugelhopf tin and small brioche moulds may be useful.
BELOW: Assorted cake tins, fluted loose-based tart tin

dough partway through the cycle, set a kitchen timer. It is also a good idea to set a timer if the beep of your bread machine is not particularly loud and you are unlikely to be in the kitchen when the signal goes off.

BANNETON

During the final proving, breads are some-times supported in cloth-lined baskets, called bannetons. Place baguettes in long bannetons and round loaves in round baskets. Flour the cloth well to prevent the dough from sticking. When the dough has risen you can up-turn the basket and place the bread directly on a prepared baking sheet.

DISHTOWELS AND CLEAR FILM (PLASTIC WRAP)

Use a clean dishtowel or clear film to cover the dough during proving to prevent a dry crust from forming. Lightly flour the dishtowel or oil the clear film to prevent the dough from sticking to the cover.

TIMER

If your bread machine does not have an audible signal to remind you to add extra ingredients, or you want to remember to check the

BAKING HAND-SHAPED LOAVES

A variety of tins (pans), trays and other equipment will help you bake breads of interesting shapes or with a crispier crust.

BREAD PANS AND MOULDS

Heavy gauge baking tins and moulds are best, because they are less likely to distort in the oven. A number of shapes and sizes are useful. A 1kg or a 2lb loaf tin mea-suring 18.5–11.5cm/7¼ × 4½in is a good basic size and shape, or try a longer, slightly narrower tin about 23–28cm/9–10in long.

Both round and square cake tins are used for bread making, to support the dough while it rises. A 15cm/6in deep cake tin is used for baking panettone.

RIGHT: Baking trays and loaf tins (pans)

BELOW: A peel is useful when making pizzas

Springform cake tins with diameters of 20–25cm/ 8–10in make the removal of sweet breads and cakes much easier than when a fixed-based cake tin is used. Square and rectangular tins are perfect for both sweet-and-savoury topped breads.

Focaccia or deep-pan pizzas are best cooked in a large, shallow, round cake tin with a diameter of 25–28cm/ 10–11in. A fluted loose-based tart pan and shallow pizza pan are good investments if you cook those types of bread regularly.

Shaped moulds are often used for baking speciality breads. A fluted mould with sloping sides is the classic shape for both individual and large brioche. Kugelhopf is made in a deep fluted tin with a central hole, savarin in a shallow ring mould and babas in shallow, individual ring moulds.

FRENCH BAGUETTE TRAY

A moulded tray, designed to hold two or three loaves, this has a perforated base to ensure an even heat while baking. The bread is given its final proving in the tray, which is then placed in the oven for baking. Loaves baked in a tray will have small dimples on the base and sides.

BAKING SHEETS

A number of free-form breads need to be transferred to a baking sheet for cooking. A selection of strong, heavy baking sheets is best. Use either totally flat baking sheets, or ones with a lip on one edge only. These make it possible to remove the cooked breads easily.

BAKING STONE

For more rustic bread, sourdoughs, pizza and focaccia, a baking stone or pizza stone helps to ensure a crisp crust.

TERRACOTTA TILES

Unglazed quarry tiles or terracotta tiles can be used instead of a baking stone. The tiles will draw out moisture and help to produce the traditional crisp crust.

PEEL

If you are regularly going to use a baking stone or tiles, a peel, sometimes called a baker's shovel, is a useful piece of equipment. Use it to slide pizzas and bread doughs into the

oven, placing them directly on to the pre-heated surface. Flour the peel generously and place the bread on it for its final proving. Give it a gentle shake just before placing it in the oven to make sure the base of the bread doesn't stick to the peel.

WATER SPRAY BOTTLE

Use a water spray bottle to mist the oven when you wish to achieve a crisp crust. A pump-action plastic bottle with a fine spray-head is ideal.

USEFUL TOOLS

This section includes tools for preparing ingredients and for finishing hand-shaped and machine breads.

CUTTERS

Plain cutters are used to cut dough for muffins and rolls. Metal cutters are best as they are not distorted when pressure is applied. A range of cutters 5–10cm/ 2–4in in diameter is most useful.

POTATO PEELER

Use a fixed-blade potato peeler for peeling vegetables and fruit, or removing strips of citrus peel. A swivel-blade peeler is useful for paring very thin layers of citrus skin.

ZESTER

Many sweet breads and cakes include fresh citrus zest and this handy little tool makes light work of preparing it. The zester has a row of holes with cutting edges which shave off thin strips of zest without including the bitter pith that lies just beneath the coloured citrus peel. You may then wish to chop the strips into smaller pieces with a very sharp knife.

PASTRY BRUSHES

These are used to apply washes and glazes. Avoid nylon brushes, which will melt if used on hot breads. Brushes made from natural fibre are better.

LEFT: A baking stone, terracotta tiles and a water spray all help to produce breads with a crispier crust.

LEFT: Selection of rolling pins

PLASTIC SCRAPER AND SPATULA

Make sure these tools are pliable. Use them to help remove dough that is stuck on the inside of the bread machine pan. The scraper also comes in handy for lifting and turning sticky dough and dividing dough into pieces for shaping into rolls.

KNIVES

You will need a sharp cook's knife for slashing doughs and a smaller paring knife for preparing fruit and vegetables. Use stainless steel for acidic fruits.

SCISSORS AND SCALPEL

Both these items can be used for slashing breads and rolls, to give decorative finishes before baking. A medium-size pair of scissors with thin, pointed blades is perfect. If you use a scalpel, replace the blade regularly, as it must be sharp.

ROLLING PINS

Some breads and buns need to be rolled out for shaping. Cylindrical wooden pins are best. Use a heavy rolling pin about 45cm/18in long for breads and a smaller one for individual rolls, buns and pastries. A child's toy rolling pin can be very useful for small items.

ABOVE: From left to right: spatula, cook's knife, vegetable knife, scalpel and scissors

THERMOMETERS

All ovens cook with slightly different heat intensities. An oven thermometer will enable you to establish how your oven cooks so you can make any necessary adjustments to recipes.

The time-honoured way of testing if a loaf of bread is cooked through is to tap it on the base to determine if it sounds hollow.

A much more scientific method is to insert a thermometer into the centre of a hand-shaped loaf and check the internal temperature. It should be 190–195°C (375–383°F).

SIEVES

A large sieve is essential for sifting flours together, and it will be handy to have one or two small sieves for sifting ingredients such as dried skimmed milk (non fat dry milk), icing (confectioners') sugar and ground spices. Use a plastic sieve for icing sugar.

COOLING AND SLICING

Cooling a bread properly gives a crispier crust. The bread is then ready to eat.

OVEN GLOVES

A thick pair of oven gloves or mitts is essential for lifting the bread pan from the machine or breads from the oven, because the metal items will be very hot.

WIRE RACK

The hot cooked bread should be turned out on to a wire rack and left to cool before storing or slicing.

BREAD KNIFE AND BOARD

To preserve the delicate crumb structure, bread should be sawn with a sharp knife that has a long serrated blade. Cut the bread on a wooden board to prevent damaging the serrated knife.

ABOVE: Oven gloves, and a wire rack for cooling bread

BASIC BREADS

These recipes are the everyday breads that you will want to make time and again. They are some of the easiest breads to make in your machine; perfect for serving toasted with lashings of butter or for use in sandwiches. They include breads made from a wide range of flours, including bulgur wheat, buckwheat and spelt, as well as breads enriched with potato or egg. If you haven't made bread in your machine before, this is the place to start.

FARMHOUSE LOAF

The flour-dusted split top gives a charmingly rustic look to this tasty wholemeal (whole-wheat) enriched white loaf.

SMALL
210ml/7½fl oz/1⅛ cup water
350g/12oz/3 cups unbleached strong
white (bread) flour, plus extra
for dusting
25g/1oz/¼ cup wholemeal
(whole-wheat bread) flour
15ml/1 tbsp skimmed milk powder
(non fat dry milk)
7.5ml/1½ tsp salt
7.5ml/1½ tsp granulated sugar
15g/½oz/1 tbsp butter
4ml/¾ tsp easy-blend (rapid-rise)
dried yeast

MEDIUM
320ml/11¼fl oz/generous 1⅓ cups water
425g/15oz/3¾ cups unbleached
strong white flour, plus extra
for dusting
75g/3oz/¾ cup strong wholemeal flour
22ml/1½ tbsp skimmed milk powder
7.5ml/1½ tsp salt
7.5ml/1½ tsp granulated sugar
25g/1oz/2 tbsp butter
5ml/1 tsp easy-blend dried yeast

LARGE
420ml/15fl oz/2 cups water
600g/1lb 5oz/5¼ cups unbleached
strong white flour, plus extra
for dusting
75g/3oz/¾ cup strong wholemeal flour
30ml/2 tbsp skimmed milk powder
10ml/2 tsp salt
10ml/2 tsp granulated sugar
25g/1oz/2 tbsp butter
7.5ml/1½ tsp easy-blend dried yeast

MAKES 1 LOAF

1 Pour the water into the bread pan. If the instructions for your bread machine specify that the yeast is to be placed in the pan first, simply reverse the order in which you add the liquid and dry ingredients.

2 Sprinkle over both the flours. Add the milk powder, and the salt, sugar and butter in separate corners. Make an indent in the flour and add the yeast.

3 Set the bread machine to the basic/normal setting, medium crust. Press Start.

4 Ten minutes before the baking time commences, brush the top of the loaf with water and dust with a little strong white (bread) flour. Slash the top of the bread with a sharp knife.

5 Remove the bread at the end of the baking cycle and turn out on to a wire rack to cool.

VARIATION
Try this rustic bread using Granary (multi-grain) flour instead of wholemeal flour for added texture.

EGG-ENRICHED WHITE LOAF

*Adding egg to a basic white loaf gives a richer flavour and creamier crumb,
as well as a golden finish to the crust.*

1 Put the egg(s) in a measuring jug (cup) and add sufficient water to give 240ml/8½fl oz/generous 1 cup, 300ml/10½fl oz/1⅓ cups or 430ml/15fl oz/scant 1⅞ cups, according to the size of loaf.

2 Mix lightly and pour into the bread machine pan. If your instructions specify that the yeast is to be placed in the pan first, reverse the order in which you add the liquid and the dry ingredients.

SMALL
1 egg
375g/13oz/3¼ cups unbleached strong
white (bread) flour
7.5ml/1½ tsp granulated sugar
7.5ml/1½ tsp salt
20g/¾oz/1½ tbsp butter
4ml/¾ tsp easy-blend (rapid-rise)
dried yeast

MEDIUM
1 egg plus 1 egg yolk
500g/1lb 2oz/4½ cups unbleached
strong white flour
10ml/2 tsp granulated sugar
7.5ml/1½ tsp salt
25g/1oz/2 tbsp butter
5ml/1 tsp easy-blend
dried yeast

LARGE
2 eggs
675g/1½lb/6 cups unbleached strong
white flour
15ml/1 tbsp granulated sugar
10ml/2 tsp salt
25g/1oz/2 tbsp butter
7.5ml/1½ tsp easy-blend
dried yeast

MAKES 1 LOAF

3 Sprinkle over the flour, covering the water. Add the sugar, salt and butter in separate corners of the pan. Make a small indent in the centre of the flour and add the yeast.

4 Set the machine to the basic/normal setting, medium crust. Press Start. At the end of the baking cycle, turn out on to a wire rack to cool.

MALTED LOAF

A malt and sultana (golden raisin) loaf makes the perfect breakfast or tea-time treat. Serve it sliced and generously spread with butter.

SMALL
200ml/7fl oz/1¼ cups water
15ml/1 tbsp golden (light corn) syrup
22ml/1½ tbsp malt extract (syrup)
350g/12oz/3 cups unbleached strong white (bread) flour
22ml/1½ tbsp skimmed milk powder (non fat dry milk)
2.5ml/½ tsp salt
40g/1½oz/3 tbsp butter
2.5ml/½ tsp easy-blend (rapid-rise) dried yeast
75g/3oz/½ cup sultanas (golden raisins)

MEDIUM
280ml/10fl oz/1½ cups water
22ml/1½ tbsp golden syrup
30ml/2 tbsp malt extract
500g/1lb 2oz/4½ cups unbleached strong white flour
30ml/2 tbsp skimmed milk powder
5ml/1 tsp salt
50g/2oz/¼ cup butter
5ml/1 tsp easy-blend dried yeast
100g/3½oz/generous ½ cup sultanas

LARGE
360ml/scant13fl oz/1¾ cups water
30ml/2 tbsp golden syrup
45ml/3 tbsp malt extract
675g/1½lb/6 cups unbleached strong white flour
30ml/2 tbsp skimmed milk powder
5ml/1 tsp salt
65g/2½oz/5 tbsp butter
7.5ml/1½ tsp easy-blend dried yeast
125g/4½oz/generous ¾ cup sultanas

MAKES 1 LOAF

1 Pour the water, syrup and malt extract into the bread machine pan. If the instructions for your machine specify that the yeast is to be placed in the pan first, reverse the order.

2 Sprinkle over the flour. Add the milk powder. Add the salt and butter in separate corners of the bread pan. Make a shallow indent in the centre of the flour and add the yeast.

3 Set the bread machine to the basic/normal setting, with raisin setting (if available), medium crust. Press Start. Add the dried fruit when the machine beeps or after the first kneading.

4 Remove at the end of the baking cycle and turn out on to a wire rack. If you like, glaze the bread. Dissolve 15ml/1 tbsp caster (superfine) sugar in 15ml/1 tbsp milk and brush over the top crust.

LIGHT WHOLEMEAL BREAD

*A tasty, light wholemeal (whole-wheat) loaf which can be cooked on the
quicker basic or normal setting.*

SMALL
*280ml/10fl oz/1½ cups water
250g/9oz/2¼ cups strong wholemeal
(whole-wheat bread) flour
125g/4½oz/1 cup strong white
(bread) flour
7.5ml/1½ tsp salt
7.5ml/1½ tsp granulated sugar
20g/¾oz/1½ tbsp butter
5ml/1 tsp easy-blend (rapid-rise)
dried yeast*

MEDIUM
*350ml/12fl oz/1¾ cups water
350g/12oz/3 cups strong wholemeal flour
150g/5½oz/1⅓ cups strong white flour
10ml/2 tsp salt
10ml/2 tsp granulated sugar
25g/1oz/2 tbsp butter
7.5ml/1½ tsp easy-blend dried yeast*

LARGE
*450ml/16fl oz/scant 2 cups water
475g/1lb 1oz/4¼ cups strong
wholemeal flour
200g/7oz/1¾ cups strong white flour
10ml/2 tsp salt
15ml/1 tbsp granulated sugar
25g/1oz/2 tbsp butter
10ml/2 tsp easy-blend dried yeast*

MAKES 1 LOAF

VARIATION
This brown loaf is a good choice for
baking in the machine as it is fairly
light, containing a mixture of white
and wholemeal flours. Another option
for a lighter brown loaf is to replace
the strong wholemeal flour with strong
brown flour. This contains less bran
and wheatgerm than wholemeal flour,
so produces a slightly lighter bread.

1 Pour the water into the bread machine
pan. If the instructions for your bread
machine specify that the yeast is to be
placed in the pan first, reverse the order
in which you add the liquid and dry
ingredients to the pan.

2 Sprinkle over each type of flour in
turn, ensuring that the water is
completely covered. Add the salt, sugar
and butter in separate corners of the
bread pan. Make a small indent in the
centre of the flour and add the yeast.

3 Set the bread machine to the
basic/normal setting, medium crust.
Press Start.

4 Remove the bread at the end of the
baking cycle and turn out on to a wire
rack to cool.

FRENCH BREAD

French bread traditionally has a crisp crust and light, chewy crumb. Use the special French bread setting on your bread machine to help to achieve this unique texture.

SMALL
MAKES 1 LOAF
150ml/5fl oz/⅔ cup water
225g/8oz/2 cups unbleached strong white (bread) flour
5ml/1 tsp salt
7.5ml/1½ tsp easy-blend (rapid-rise) dried yeast

MEDIUM
MAKES 2–3 LOAVES
315ml/11fl oz/1⅓ cups water
450g/1lb/4 cups unbleached strong white flour
7.5ml/1½ tsp salt
7.5ml/1½ tsp easy-blend dried yeast

LARGE
MAKES 3–4 LOAVES
500ml/17½fl oz/2⅛ cups water
675g/1½lb/6 cups unbleached strong white flour
10ml/2 tsp salt
10ml/2 tsp easy-blend dried yeast

1 Add the water to the bread machine pan. If the instructions for your machine specify that the yeast is to be placed in the pan first, simply reverse the order in which you add the ingredients.

2 Sprinkle over the flour, to cover the water. Add the salt in a corner. Make an indent in the centre of the flour and add the yeast. Use the French bread dough setting (see Cook's Tip). Press Start.

3 When the dough cycle has finished, remove the dough from the machine, place it on a lightly floured surface and knock it back (punch down). Divide it into two or three equal portions if using the medium quantities or three or four portions if using the large quantities.

4 On a floured surface shape each piece of dough into a ball, then roll out to a rectangle measuring 18–20 × 7.5cm/ 7–8 × 3in. Fold one-third up lengthways and one-third down, then press. Repeat twice more, leaving the dough to rest between foldings to avoid tearing.

5 Gently roll and stretch each piece to a 28–33cm/11–13in loaf, depending on whether you aim to make smaller or larger loaves. Place each loaf in a floured banneton or between the folds of a floured and pleated dishtowel, so that the French bread shape is maintained during rising.

6 Cover with lightly oiled clear film (plastic wrap) and leave in a warm place for 30–45 minutes. Preheat the oven to 230°C/450°F/Gas 8.

7 Roll the loaf or loaves on to a baking sheet. Slash the tops several times with a knife. Place at the top of the oven, spray the inside of the oven with water and bake for 15–20 minutes, or until golden. Transfer to a wire rack to cool.

COOK'S TIP
Use the French bread baking setting if you do not have a French bread dough setting. Remove the dough before the final rising stage and shape as directed.

POTATO BREAD

This golden crusty loaf has a moist soft centre and is perfect for sandwiches.
Use the water in which the potatoes have been cooked to make this bread.
If you haven't got enough, make up the remainder with tap water.

1 Pour the water and sunflower oil into the bread machine pan. However, if the instructions for your machine specify that the yeast is to be placed in the pan first, reverse the order in which you add the liquid and dry ingredients.

2 Sprinkle over the flour, ensuring that it covers the water. Add the mashed potato and milk powder. Add the salt and sugar in separate corners of the bread pan. Make a small indent in the centre of the flour (but not down as far as the liquid) and add the yeast.

3 Set the bread machine to the basic/normal setting, medium crust. Press Start. To glaze the loaf, brush the top with milk either at the beginning of the cooking time or halfway through.

4 Remove the bread at the end of the baking cycle and turn out on to a wire rack to cool.

SMALL
200ml/7fl oz/⅞ cup potato cooking water, at room temperature
30ml/2 tbsp sunflower oil
375g/13oz/3¼ cups unbleached strong white (bread) flour
125g/4½oz/1½ cups cold cooked mashed potato
15ml/1 tbsp skimmed milk powder (non fat dry milk)
5ml/1 tsp salt
7.5ml/1½ tsp granulated sugar
5ml/1 tsp easy-blend (rapid-rise) dried yeast
milk, for glazing

MEDIUM
225ml/8fl oz/scant 1 cup potato cooking water, at room temperature
45ml/3 tbsp sunflower oil
500g/1lb 2oz/4½ cups unbleached strong white flour
175g/6oz/2 cups cold mashed potato
22ml/1½ tbsp skimmed milk powder
7.5ml/1½ tsp salt
10ml/2 tsp granulated sugar
7.5ml/1½ tsp easy-blend dried yeast
milk, for glazing

LARGE
330ml/11½fl oz/scant 1½ cups potato cooking water, at room temperature
60ml/4 tbsp sunflower oil
675g/1½lb/6 cups unbleached strong white flour
225g/8oz/2⅔ cups cold mashed potato
30ml/2 tbsp skimmed milk powder
10ml/2 tsp salt
15ml/1 tbsp granulated sugar
7.5ml/1½ tsp easy-blend dried yeast
milk, for glazing

MAKES 1 LOAF

COOK'S TIP
If using leftover potatoes mashed with milk and butter you may need to reduce the liquid a little. If making the mashed potato, use 175g/6oz, 200g/7oz or 275g/10oz raw potatoes, depending on machine size.

MAIZEMEAL BREAD

Maizemeal (cornmeal) adds a sweet flavour and crumbly texture to this scrumptious bread. Use a finely ground meal from the health-food shop. The coarsely ground meal used for polenta makes a good topping.

SMALL
150ml/5fl oz/⅔ cup water
75ml/2½fl oz/6 tbsp milk
15ml/1 tbsp corn oil
275g/10oz/2½ cups unbleached strong white (bread) flour
100g/3½oz/scant 1 cup maizemeal (cornmeal)
5ml/1 tsp salt
7.5ml/1½ tsp light muscovado (molasses) sugar
5ml/1 tsp easy-blend (rapid-rise) dried yeast
water, for glazing
polenta, for sprinkling

MEDIUM
210ml/7½fl oz/1 cup water
90ml/3fl oz/7 tbsp milk
22ml/1½ tbsp corn oil
350g/12½oz/3 cups unbleached strong white flour
150g/5oz/1¼ cups maizemeal
5ml/1 tsp salt
10ml/2 tsp light muscovado sugar
5ml/1 tsp easy-blend dried yeast
water, for glazing
polenta, for sprinkling

LARGE
250ml/9fl oz/generous 1¼ cups water
150ml/5fl oz/⅔ cup milk
30ml/2 tbsp corn oil
450g/1lb/4 cups unbleached strong white flour
225g/8oz/2 cups maizemeal
7.5ml/1½ tsp salt
15ml/1 tbsp light muscovado sugar
7.5ml/1½ tsp easy-blend dried yeast
water, for glazing
polenta, for sprinkling

MAKES 1 LOAF

COOK'S TIP

This bread is best cooked on a rapid setting, even though the inclusion of maizemeal will result in a slightly shallow loaf. Maizemeal (sometimes known as cornmeal) is available from most health food shops.

1 Pour the water, milk and corn oil into the pan. Reverse the order in which you add the wet and dry ingredients if the instructions to your machine specify this.

2 Add the flour and the maizemeal (cornmeal), covering the water. Place the salt and sugar in separate corners. Make a shallow indent in the flour; add the yeast.

3 Set the bread machine to the rapid/quick setting, medium crust. Press Start. Just before the baking cycle commences brush the top of the loaf with water and sprinkle with polenta.

4 Remove the bread at the end of the baking cycle and turn out on to a wire rack to cool.

POLENTA AND WHOLEMEAL LOAF

Polenta adds an interesting grainy quality to the texture of this rich wholemeal (whole-wheat) bread, which is perfect for everyday use.

SMALL

220ml/scant 8fl oz/1¼ cups water
30ml/2 tbsp clear honey
25g/1oz/2 tbsp polenta
25g/1oz/¼ cup unbleached strong
white (bread) flour
325g/11½oz/scant 3 cups wholemeal
(whole-wheat bread) flour
5ml/1 tsp salt
20g/¾oz/1½ tbsp butter
4ml/¾ tsp easy-blend (rapid-rise)
dried yeast

MEDIUM

300ml/10½fl oz/1¼ cups water
45ml/3 tbsp clear honey
50g/2oz/scant ½ cup polenta
50g/2oz/½ cup unbleached strong
white flour
400g/14oz/3½ cups strong
wholemeal flour
7.5ml/1½ tsp salt
25g/1oz/2 tbsp butter
7.5ml/1½ tsp easy-blend dried yeast

LARGE

350ml/12fl oz/1½ cups water
60ml/4 tbsp clear honey
75g/3oz/scant ¾ cup polenta
75g/3oz/¾ cup unbleached strong
white flour
525g/1lb 3oz/4¾ cups strong
wholemeal flour
10ml/2 tsp salt
40g/1½oz/3 tbsp butter
10ml/2 tsp easy-blend dried yeast

MAKES 1 LOAF

1 Add the water and honey to the pan. If necessary, reverse the order in which you add the liquid and dry ingredients. Sprinkle over the polenta and flours, ensuring that the liquid is covered.

2 Add the salt and butter in separate corners of the pan. Make a small indent in the centre of the flour (but not down as far as the liquid) and add the yeast.

3 Set the machine to the whole wheat setting, medium crust. Press Start.

COOK'S TIP
This bread is perfect for breakfast and it may be baked using the automatic delay timer. The small quantity of butter should be fine overnight, but if you wish, substitute vegetable oil and adjust the liquid accordingly.

4 Remove the loaf from the bread pan at the end of the baking cycle and turn out on to a wire rack to cool.

SPELT AND BULGUR WHEAT BREAD

Two unusual grains are used here. Spelt is a variety of wheat which is not widely grown, but is ground by some specialist millers. Cracked wheat or bulgur is the cracked wheat berry which has been softened by steaming. It contributes crunch while the spelt flour adds a nutty flavour.

VARIATION
The buttermilk adds a characteristic slightly sour note to this bread. You can replace it with natural (plain) yogurt or semi-skimmed (low-fat) milk for a less pronounced flavour.

1 Pour the water, buttermilk and lemon juice into the bread machine pan. If the instructions for your machine specify that the yeast is to be placed in the pan first, reverse the order in which you add the liquid and dry ingredients.

2 Sprinkle over both types of flour, then the bulgur wheat, ensuring that the liquid is completely covered. Add the salt and sugar, placing them in separate corners of the bread pan.

3 Make a small indent in the centre of the flour (but not down as far as the liquid) and add the yeast.

4 Set the bread machine to the basic/normal setting, medium crust. Press Start.

5 Remove the bread at the end of the baking cycle and turn out on to a wire rack to allow to cool.

BUCKWHEAT AND WALNUT BREAD

Buckwheat flour is made from toasted buckwheat groats. It has a distinctive earthy taste, perfectly mellowed when blended with white flour and walnuts in this compact bread, flavoured with molasses.

SMALL

210ml/7½fl oz/1⅛ cups water
10ml/2 tsp molasses
22ml/1½ tbsp walnut or olive oil
315g/11oz/2¾ cups unbleached strong white (bread) flour
50g/2oz/½ cup buckwheat flour
15ml/1 tbsp skimmed milk powder (non fat dry milk)
5ml/1 tsp salt
2.5ml/½ tsp granulated sugar
5ml/1 tsp easy-blend (rapid-rise) dried yeast
40g/1½oz/⅓ cup walnut pieces

MEDIUM

315ml/11fl oz/1⅓ cups water
15ml/3 tsp molasses
30ml/2 tbsp walnut or olive oil
425g/15oz/3¾ cups unbleached strong white flour
75g/3oz/¾ cup buckwheat flour
22ml/1½ tbsp skimmed milk powder
7.5ml/1½ tsp salt
4ml/¾ tsp granulated sugar
5ml/1 tsp easy-blend dried yeast
50g/2oz/½ cup walnut pieces

LARGE

420ml/15fl oz/generous 1¾ cups water
20ml/4 tsp molasses
45ml/3 tbsp walnut or olive oil
575g/1¼lb/5 cups unbleached strong white flour
115g/4oz/1 cup buckwheat flour
30ml/2 tbsp skimmed milk powder
10ml/2 tsp salt
5ml/1 tsp granulated sugar
7.5ml/1½ tsp easy-blend dried yeast
75g/3oz/¾ cup walnut pieces

MAKES 1 LOAF

3 Set the bread machine to the basic/normal setting; use raisin setting (if available), medium crust. Press Start. Add the nut pieces when the machine beeps or after the first kneading.

4 Remove the bread from the pan at the end of the baking cycle and turn out on to a wire rack to cool.

1 Pour the water, molasses and walnut or olive oil into the bread pan. If the instructions for your machine specify that the yeast is to be placed in the pan first, reverse the order in which you add the liquid and dry ingredients.

2 Sprinkle over the flours, covering the liquid. Add the milk powder. Place the salt and sugar in separate corners. Make a small indent in the centre of the flour (but not down as far as the liquid) and add the easy-blend dried yeast.

MUESLI AND DATE BREAD

260ml/9fl oz/scant 1⅛ cups water
30ml/2 tbsp sunflower oil
15ml/1 tbsp clear honey
300g/10½oz/2⅔ cups unbleached
strong white (bread) flour
75g/3oz/¾ cup wholemeal
(whole-wheat bread) flour
150g/5½oz/generous 1½ cups
unsweetened muesli (granola)
45ml/3 tbsp skimmed milk powder
(non fat dry milk)
7.5ml/1½ tsp salt
7.5ml/1½ tsp easy-blend (rapid-rise)
dried yeast
65g/2½oz/scant ½ cup stoned (pitted)
dates, chopped

MAKES 1 LOAF

This makes the perfect breakfast or brunch bread. Use your own favourite unsweetened muesli for your own individual version.

1 Pour the water, oil and honey into the pan. Reverse the order if necessary. Sprinkle over the flours. Add the muesli and milk, then the salt, in a corner. Make an indent and add the yeast.

2 Set the bread machine to the dough setting; use basic raisin dough setting (if available). Press Start. Add the dates when the machine beeps or during the last 5 minutes of kneading. Lightly oil a baking sheet.

3 When the dough cycle has finished, remove the dough and place it on a surface dusted with wholemeal flour. Knock it back (punch it down) gently.

4 Shape the dough into a plump round and place it on the prepared baking sheet. Using a sharp knife make three cuts on the top about 1cm/½in deep, to divide the bread into six sections.

5 Cover with lightly oiled clear film (plastic wrap) and leave to rise for 30–45 minutes, until doubled in size.

6 Preheat the oven to 200°C/400°F/ Gas 6. Bake the loaf for 30–35 minutes until it is golden and hollow sounding. Transfer it to a wire rack to cool.

COOK'S TIP
The amount of water required may vary with the type of muesli used. Add another 15ml/1 tbsp water if the dough is too firm.

BARLEY-ENRICHED FARMHOUSE LOAF

260ml/9fl oz/1⅛ cups water
45ml/3 tbsp double (heavy) cream
400g/14oz/3½ cups unbleached strong
white (bread) flour
115g/4oz/1 cup barley flour
10ml/2 tsp granulated sugar
10ml/2 tsp salt
7.5ml/1½ tsp easy-blend (rapid-rise)
dried yeast
25g/1oz/2 tbsp pumpkin seeds
flour, for dusting

MAKES 1 LOAF

Barley adds a very distinctive, earthy, slightly nutty flavour to this crusty white loaf.

1 Pour the water and cream into the pan. Reverse the order in which you add the liquid and dry ingredients if necessary. Sprinkle over both types of flour, covering the water completely.

2 Add the sugar and salt, placing them in separate corners of the pan. Make a shallow indent in the centre of the flour and add the yeast.

3 Set the bread machine to the dough setting; use basic raisin dough setting (if available). Press Start. Add the pumpkin seeds when the machine beeps or during the last 5 minutes of kneading. Lightly oil a 900g/2lb loaf tin (pan) measuring 18.5 × 12cm/7¼ × 4½in.

4 When the dough cycle has finished, remove the dough from the machine and place on a lightly floured surface. Knock back (punch down) gently. Shape the dough into a rectangle, making the longer side the same length as the tin.

5 Roll the dough up lengthways, and tuck the ends under. Place it in the tin, with the seam underneath. Cover with lightly oiled clear film (plastic wrap) and leave to rise for 30–45 minutes, or until the dough reaches the top of the tin.

6 Dust the loaf with flour then make a deep lengthways cut along the top. Leave to rest for 10 minutes. Preheat the oven to 220°C/425°F/Gas 7.

7 Bake the loaf for 15 minutes, then reduce the oven temperature to 200°C/ 400°F/Gas 6 and bake for 20–25 minutes more, or until the bread is golden and sounds hollow when tapped on the base. Transfer it to a wire rack to cool.

BRAN AND YOGURT BREAD

This soft-textured yogurt bread is enriched with bran. It is high in fibre and makes wonderful toast.

SMALL
150ml/5fl oz/1 cup water
125ml/4½fl oz/generous ½ cup
natural (plain) yogurt
15ml/1 tbsp sunflower oil
15ml/1 tbsp molasses
200g/7oz/1¾ cups unbleached strong
white (bread) flour
150g/5½oz/1⅓ cups wholemeal
(whole-wheat bread) flour
25g/1oz/⅓ cup wheat bran
5ml/1 tsp salt
4ml/¾ tsp easy-blend (rapid-rise)
dried yeast

MEDIUM
185ml/6½fl oz/1¼ cups water
175ml/6fl oz/¾ cup natural yogurt
22ml/1½ tbsp sunflower oil
30ml/2 tbsp molasses
260g/generous 9oz/2⅓ cups
unbleached strong white flour
200g/7oz/1¾ cups strong
wholemeal flour
40g/1½oz/½ cup wheat bran
7.5ml/1½ tsp salt
5ml/1 tsp easy-blend dried yeast

LARGE
230ml/8fl oz/1⅓ cups water
210ml/7½fl oz/scant 1 cup
natural yogurt
30ml/2 tbsp sunflower oil
30ml/2 tbsp molasses
375g/13oz/3¼ cups unbleached strong
white flour
250g/9oz/2¼ cups strong
wholemeal flour
50g/2oz/⅔ cup wheat bran
10ml/2 tsp salt
7.5ml/1½ tsp easy-blend dried yeast

MAKES 1 LOAF

COOK'S TIP
Molasses is added to this bread to give added flavour and colour. You can use treacle or golden (light corn) syrup instead, to intensify or lessen the flavour respectively, if desired.

1 Pour the water, yogurt, oil and molasses into the bread machine pan. If the instructions for your machine specify that the yeast is to be placed in the pan first, reverse the order in which you add the liquid and dry ingredients.

2 Sprinkle over both the white and the wholemeal flours, ensuring that the liquid mixture is completely covered. Add the wheat bran and salt, then make a small indent in the centre of the dry ingredients (but not down as far as the liquid) and add the easy-blend dried yeast.

3 Set the bread machine to the basic/normal setting, medium crust. Press Start.

4 Remove the bread from the pan at the end of the baking cycle and turn out on to a wire rack to cool. Serve when still just warm, if you like.

MAPLE AND OATMEAL LOAF

Rolled oats and oat bran add texture to this wholesome bread, which is suffused with the delectable flavour of maple syrup.

SMALL
210ml/7½fl oz/scant 1 cup water
15ml/1 tbsp maple syrup
300g/10½oz/3¾ cups unbleached strong white (bread) flour
50g/2oz/½ cup wholemeal (whole-wheat bread) flour
20g/¾oz/¼ cup rolled oats
15ml/1 tbsp oat bran
5ml/1 tsp salt
5ml/1 tsp granulated sugar
25g/1oz/2 tbsp butter
5ml/1 tsp easy-blend (rapid-rise) dried yeast

MEDIUM
315ml/11fl oz/1⅓ cups water
30ml/2 tbsp maple syrup
375g/13oz/3¼ cups unbleached strong white flour
75g/3oz/¾ cup strong wholemeal flour
40g/1½oz/½ cup rolled oats
30ml/2 tbsp oat bran
5ml/1 tsp salt
5ml/1 tsp granulated sugar
40g/1½oz/3 tbsp butter
5ml/1 tsp easy-blend dried yeast

LARGE
410ml/14½fl oz/1¾ cups water
45ml/3 tbsp maple syrup
500g/1lb 2oz/4½ cups unbleached strong white flour
115g/4oz/1 cup strong wholemeal flour
50g/2oz/⅔ cup rolled oats
45ml/3 tbsp oat bran
7.5ml/1½ tsp salt
7.5ml/1½ tsp granulated sugar
50g/2oz/¼ cup butter
7.5ml/1½ tsp easy-blend dried yeast

MAKES 1 LOAF

1 Pour the water into the bread machine pan and then add the maple syrup. If the instructions for your machine specify that the yeast is to be placed in the pan first, reverse the order in which you add the liquid and dry ingredients.

2 Sprinkle over both the white and wholemeal flours, then the rolled oats and oat bran, ensuring that the water is completely covered.

3 Add the salt, sugar and butter, placing them in separate corners of the bread pan. Make a small indent in the centre of the flour (but not down as far as the liquid) and add the yeast.

4 Set the bread machine to the basic/normal setting, medium crust. Press Start.

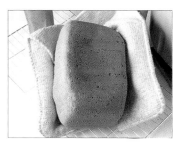

5 Remove the bread at the end of the baking cycle and turn out on to a wire rack to cool.

COOK'S TIP
Use 100 per cent pure maple syrup. Less expensive products are often blended with cane or corn syrup, which does not have the smooth rich flavour of the real thing.

SAVOURY BREADS

Adding flavourings to a basic dough provides many new ideas. Herbs, such as rosemary, dill and sage, along with garlic and onion will fill the kitchen with delicious scents. Cheeses such as mascarpone, Parmesan, Gorgonzola and mozzarella can be used to give rich loaves with a wonderful aroma. You can also add meat or cooked vegetables to savoury breads for a tasty flavour: try pumpkin, sweet potato or sun-dried tomatoes.

STROMBOLI

This variation on Italian focaccia takes its name from the volcanic island of Stromboli, near Sicily. The dough is pierced to allow the filling to "erupt" through the holes during baking. This bread can be served warm or cold.

200ml/7fl oz/⅞ cup water
350g/12oz/3 cups strong unbleached white (bread) flour
2.5ml/½ tsp granulated sugar
5ml/1 tsp salt
5ml/1 tsp easy-blend (rapid rise) dried yeast

FOR THE FILLING
175g/6oz mozzarella cheese, grated or finely chopped
75g/3oz/1 cup freshly grated Parmesan cheese
15ml/1 tbsp chopped fresh flat leaf parsley
30ml/2 tbsp fresh basil leaves
5ml/1 tsp freshly ground black pepper
1 garlic clove, finely chopped

FOR THE TOPPING
15ml/1 tbsp extra virgin olive oil
4–5 small fresh rosemary sprigs

MAKES 1 LOAF

1 Pour the water into the machine pan. Reverse the order in which you add the wet and dry ingredients if necessary. Sprinkle over the flour, ensuring that it covers the water. Add the sugar and salt in separate corners of the pan. Make a shallow indent in the centre of the flour and add the yeast.

2 Set the bread machine to the dough setting; use basic dough setting (if available). Press Start.

3 Oil a baking sheet.When the dough cycle has ended, remove the dough and place on a floured surface. Knock it back (punch it down) gently. Roll out into a rectangle measuring 30 × 23cm/12 × 9in. Cover with oiled clear film (plastic wrap) and leave to rest for 5 minutes.

4 Sprinkle over the cheeses leaving a 1cm/½in clear border along each edge. Add the parsley, basil, pepper and garlic.

5 Starting from a shorter side, roll up the dough, Swiss (jelly) roll fashion, tucking the side edges under to seal. Place the roll, seam down, on the baking sheet. Cover with lightly oiled clear film (plastic wrap) and leave in a warm place for 30 minutes, or until the dough roll has almost doubled in size.

6 Preheat the oven to 200°C/400°F/ Gas 6. Brush the top of the bread with olive oil, then prick holes in the bread with a skewer, from the top right through to the base. Sprinkle over the rosemary. Bake for 30–35 minutes, or until golden. Transfer it to a wire rack.

THREE CHEESES BREAD

A tempting trio of Italian cheeses – mascarpone, Gorgonzola and Parmesan – are responsible for the marvellous flavour of this round loaf.

180ml/6½fl oz/generous ¾ cup water
1 egg
100g/3½oz/5 tbsp mascarpone cheese
400g/14oz/3½ cups strong unbleached white (bread) flour
50g/2oz/½ cup Granary (multi-grain) flour
10ml/2 tsp granulated sugar
5ml/1 tsp salt
7.5ml/1½ tsp easy-blend (rapid-rise) dried yeast
75g/3oz Mountain Gorgonzola cheese, cut into small dice
75g/3oz/1 cup freshly grated Parmesan cheese
45ml/3 tbsp chopped fresh chives

FOR THE TOPPING
1 egg yolk
15ml/1 tbsp water
15ml/1 tbsp wheat flakes

MAKES 1 LOAF

1 Add the water, egg and mascarpone to the pan. Reverse the order in which you add the wet and dry ingredients if necessary. Sprinkle over both types of flour, covering the water completely.

2 Add the sugar and salt in separate corners. Make a small indent in the flour; add the yeast. Set the machine to the dough setting; use basic raisin dough setting (if available). Press Start.

3 Add the Gorgonzola, Parmesan and chives as the machine beeps or during the last 5 minutes of kneading. Lightly oil a baking sheet.

4 When the cycle has finished, place the dough on a floured surface. Knock back (punch down) gently, then shape it into a round loaf, 20cm/8in in diameter.

5 Cover with oiled clear film (plastic wrap); leave to rise in a warm place for 30–45 minutes.

6 Preheat the oven to 200°C/400°F/ Gas 6. Mix the egg yolk and water and brush over the top of the bread. Sprinkle with wheat flakes. Score the top of the bread into eight segments. Bake for 30–35 minutes, or until golden. Turn out on to a wire rack to cool.

VENISON TORDU

This pretty twisted bread is punctuated with strips of smoked venison, black pepper and crushed juniper berries. It tastes delicious on its own, perhaps with a glass of red wine. Alternatively, cut the bread into thick slices and serve it with olives and nuts as a precursor to an Italian meal.

230ml/8fl oz/1 cup water
350g/12oz/3 cups strong unbleached white (bread) flour, plus extra for dusting
5ml/1 tsp granulated sugar
5ml/1 tsp salt
5ml/1 tsp easy-blend (rapid-rise) dried yeast
40g/1½oz smoked venison, cut into strips
5ml/1 tsp freshly ground black pepper
5ml/1 tsp juniper berries, crushed

MAKES 1 LOAF

1 Pour the water into the bread machine pan. If the instructions for your bread machine specify that the yeast is to be placed in the pan first, simply reverse the order in which you add the liquid and dry ingredients to the pan.

2 Sprinkle over the strong white flour, ensuring that it completely covers the water. Add the sugar and salt, placing them in separate corners of the bread pan. Make a shallow indent in the centre of the flour (but not down as far as the liquid) and add the easy-blend dried yeast.

3 Set the bread machine to the dough setting; use basic dough setting (if available). Press Start. Meanwhile, lightly oil a baking sheet.

4 When the dough cycle has finished, remove the dough from the bread machine pan and place it on a lightly floured surface. Knock it back (punch it down) gently. Shape the dough into a ball and flatten the top slightly.

5 Roll the dough out to a round, about 2cm/¾in thick. Sprinkle the top of the dough with venison strips, black pepper and juniper berries. Leave a 1cm/½in clear border around the edge.

6 Fold one side of the dough to the centre, then repeat on the other side.

7 Press the folds gently with a rolling pin to seal them, then fold again along the centre line.

COOK'S TIP
Try using cured and smoked venison, marinated in olive oil and herbs, for this recipe. The olive oil and herbs add an extra flavour which beautifully complements this bread. Alternatively, sprinkle 5ml/1 tsp of dried herbs such as rosemary, thyme, sage or oregano over the dough in step 4.

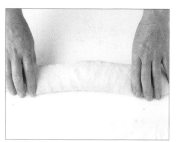

8 Press the seam gently to seal, then roll the dough backwards and forwards to make a loaf about 65cm/26in long.

9 Using the side of your hand, press across the centre of the loaf to make an indentation. Bring both ends towards each other to make an upside down "U" shape and twist together.

10 Place the venison tordu on the prepared baking sheet. Cover the loaf with lightly oiled clear film (plastic wrap) and leave to rise in a warm place for 30 minutes, or until it has almost doubled in size. Meanwhile, preheat the oven to 220°C/425°F/Gas 7. Remove the clear film and dust the top of the twisted loaf with white flour.

11 Bake for 25–30 minutes, or until the bread is golden and sounds hollow when tapped on the base. Turn out on to a wire rack to cool. Serve freshly baked, while the bread is still slightly warm.

CHICKPEA AND PEPPERCORN BREAD

Bread may be a basic food, but it certainly isn't boring, as this exciting combination proves. Chickpeas help to keep the dough light, while pink and green peppercorns add colour and "explosions" of flavour.

SMALL

200ml/7fl oz/1⅛ cups water
15ml/1 tbsp extra virgin olive oil
125g/4½oz/generous ⅔ cup canned chickpeas
375g/13oz/3¼ cups strong unbleached white (bread) flour
7.5ml/1½ tsp drained fresh pink peppercorns in brine
7.5ml/1½ tsp drained fresh green peppercorns in brine
15ml/1 tbsp skimmed milk powder (non fat dry milk)
5ml/1 tsp salt
7.5ml/1½ tsp granulated sugar
5ml/1 tsp easy-blend (rapid-rise) dried yeast
milk, for brushing (optional)

MEDIUM

250ml/9fl oz/generous 1½ cups water
30ml/2 tbsp extra virgin olive oil
175g/6oz/1 cup canned chickpeas
500g/1lb 2oz/4½ cups unbleached strong white flour
10ml/2 tsp drained fresh pink peppercorns in brine
10ml/2 tsp drained fresh green peppercorns in brine
22ml/1½ tbsp skimmed milk powder
7.5ml/1½ tsp salt
10ml/2 tsp granulated sugar
7.5ml/1½ tsp easy-blend dried yeast
milk, for brushing (optional)

LARGE

330ml/11½fl oz/1¾ cups water
45ml/3 tbsp extra virgin olive oil
225g/8oz/1⅓ cups canned chickpeas
675g/1½lb/6 cups unbleached strong white flour
15ml/1 tbsp drained fresh pink peppercorns in brine
15ml/1 tbsp drained fresh green peppercorns in brine
30ml/2 tbsp skimmed milk powder
10ml/2 tsp salt
15ml/1 tbsp granulated sugar
7.5ml/1½ tsp easy-blend dried yeast
milk, for brushing (optional)

MAKES 1 LOAF

1 Pour the water and olive oil into the bread pan. Drain the canned chickpeas well and add them to the liquid. If the instructions for your bread machine specify that the yeast is to be placed in the pan first, then reverse the order in which you add the liquid and dry ingredients to the bread pan.

2 Sprinkle over the flour, ensuring that it covers the ingredients already placed in the pan. Add the pink and green peppercorns and milk powder.

3 Place the salt and sugar in separate corners of the pan. Make a small indent in the centre of the flour (but not down as far as the liquid) and add the yeast.

4 Set the bread machine to the basic/normal setting, medium crust. Press Start. If you like, brush the top of the loaf with milk just before the bread starts to bake.

5 Remove the bread at the end of the baking cycle and turn out on to a wire rack to cool.

GARLIC AND HERB WALNUT BREAD

Walnut bread is very popular in France. This variation includes both garlic and basil for additional flavour.

1 Pour the milk, water and olive oil into the bread machine pan. If the instructions for your machine specify that the yeast is to be placed in the pan first, reverse the order in which you add the liquid and dry ingredients.

2 Sprinkle over the flour and rolled oats, ensuring that they completely cover the liquid mixture. Add the chopped walnuts, garlic, oregano and basil. Place the salt and sugar in separate corners of the bread machine pan. Make a small indent in the centre of the flour (but do not go down as far as the liquid) and add the easy-blend dried yeast.

3 Set the bread machine to the basic/normal setting, medium crust, then press Start.

4 Remove the bread at the end of the baking cycle and turn out on to a wire rack to cool.

SMALL
150ml/5fl oz/⅔ cup milk
60ml/2fl oz/¼ cup water
30ml/2 tbsp extra virgin olive oil
325g/11½oz/scant 3 cups strong
unbleached white (bread) flour
40g/1½oz/scant ⅛ cup rolled oats
40g/1½oz/⅓ cup chopped walnuts
1 garlic clove, finely chopped
5ml/1 tsp dried oregano
5ml/1 tsp drained fresh basil in
sunflower oil
5ml/1 tsp salt
7.5ml/1½ tsp granulated sugar
2.5ml/½ tsp easy-blend (rapid-rise)
dried yeast

MEDIUM
185ml/6½fl oz/generous ¾ cup milk
105ml/7 tbsp/½ cup water
45ml/3 tbsp extra virgin olive oil
450g/1lb/4 cups unbleached strong
white flour
50g/2oz/½ cup rolled oats
50g/2oz/½ cup chopped walnuts
1½ garlic cloves, finely chopped
7.5ml/1½ tsp dried oregano
7.5ml/1½ tsp drained fresh basil in
sunflower oil
7.5ml/1½ tsp salt
10ml/2 tsp granulated sugar
5ml/1 tsp easy-blend dried yeast

LARGE
200ml/7fl oz/scant 1 cup milk
140ml/5fl oz/⅔ cup water
60ml/4 tbsp extra virgin olive oil
600g/1lb 5oz/generous 5¼ cups
unbleached strong white flour
65g/2½oz/scant ⅔ cup rolled oats
65g/2½oz/generous ½ cup
chopped walnuts
2 garlic cloves, finely chopped
7.5ml/1½ tsp dried oregano
7.5ml/1½ tsp drained fresh basil in
sunflower oil
10ml/2 tsp salt
10ml/2 tsp granulated sugar
7.5ml/1½ tsp easy-blend dried yeast

MAKES 1 LOAF

SWEET POTATO BREAD

Adding sweet potato to the dough creates a loaf with a rich golden crust and the crumb is beautifully moist. Make sure you use the deep yellow sweet potatoes, in preference to the white variety of sweet potatoes, to give the bread a lovely colour.

SMALL

175g/6oz sweet potatoes, peeled
190ml/6⅓fl oz/scant ⅞ cup water
350g/12oz/3 cups strong unbleached white (bread) flour
30ml/2 tbsp rolled oats
22ml/1½ tbsp skimmed milk powder (non fat dry milk)
5ml/1 tsp salt
15ml/1 tbsp muscovado (molasses) sugar
25g/1oz/2 tbsp butter
5ml/1 tsp easy-blend (rapid-rise) dried yeast

FOR THE TOPPING
5ml/1 tsp rolled oats
5ml/1 tsp wheat grain

MEDIUM

225g/8oz sweet potatoes, peeled
210ml/7½fl oz/scant 1 cup water
500g/1lb 2oz/4½ cups unbleached strong white flour
45ml/3 tbsp rolled oats
30ml/2 tbsp skimmed milk powder
7.5ml/1½ tsp salt
22ml/1½ tbsp muscovado sugar
40g/1½oz/3 tbsp butter
7.5ml/1½ tsp easy-blend dried yeast

FOR THE TOPPING
10ml/2 tsp rolled oats
10ml/2 tsp wheat grain

LARGE

350g/12oz sweet potatoes, peeled
320ml/11¼fl oz/scant 1⅜ cups water
675g/1½lb/6 cups unbleached strong white flour
60ml/4 tbsp rolled oats
30ml/2 tbsp skimmed milk powder
7.5ml/1½ tsp salt
22ml/1½ tbsp muscovado sugar
50g/2oz/¼ cup butter
7.5ml/1½ tsp easy-blend dried yeast

FOR THE TOPPING
15ml/1 tbsp rolled oats
15ml/1 tbsp wheat grain

MAKES 1 LOAF

1 Cook the sweet potato in plenty of boiling water for 40 minutes or until very tender. Drain, and when cool enough to handle, peel off the skin. Place the sweet potato in a large bowl and mash well, but do not add any butter or milk.

2 Pour the water into the bread machine pan. However, if the instructions for your bread machine specify that the yeast is to be placed in the bread pan first, simply reverse the order in which you add the liquid and dry ingredients.

VARIATION

This bread is a good opportunity to use up any leftover sweet potato. If the potato has been mashed with milk and butter you may need to reduce the quantity of liquid a little. Use the following quantities of cooked, mashed sweet potatoes:
small machine: 125g/4½oz/1½ cups
medium machine: 175g/6oz/2 cups
large machine: 225g/8oz/2⅔ cups

COOK'S TIP

Rolled oats add a chewy texture and nutty taste to this loaf of bread. Make sure you use the traditional old-fashioned rolled oats, rather than "quick cook" oats.

3 Sprinkle the strong white flour, rolled oats and skimmed milk powder over the water, covering it completely. Weigh or measure the cooked sweet potatoes to ensure the quantity matches the amount given in the variation box (below). Then add the potatoes to the bread pan.

4 Place the salt, sugar and butter in three separate corners of the bread machine pan. Make a shallow indent in the flour (but not down as far as the liquid underneath) and add the easy-blend dried yeast.

5 Set the bread machine to the basic/normal setting, medium crust. Press Start.

6 When the rising cycle is almost complete, just before the bread begins to bake, add the topping: brush the top of the loaf with a little water and sprinkle the rolled oats and wheat grain over the top of the bread.

7 Remove the bread at the end of the baking cycle and turn out on to a wire rack to cool.

Sun-dried Tomato Bread

The dense texture and highly concentrated flavour of sun-dried tomatoes makes them perfect for flavouring bread dough, and when Parmesan cheese is added, the result is an exceptionally tasty loaf.

SMALL
15g/½oz/¼ cup sun-dried tomatoes
130ml/4½fl oz/⅗ cup water
70ml/2½fl oz/⅓ cup milk
15ml/1 tbsp extra virgin olive oil
325g/11½oz/scant 3 cups strong
unbleached white (bread) flour
50g/2oz/½ cup strong wholemeal
(whole-wheat bread) flour
40g/1½oz/½ cup freshly grated
Parmesan cheese
5ml/1 tsp salt
5ml/1 tsp granulated sugar
4ml/¾ tsp easy-blend (rapid-rise)
dried yeast

MEDIUM
25g/1oz/½ cup sun-dried tomatoes
190ml/6¾fl oz/1 cup water
115ml/4fl oz/½ cup milk
30ml/2 tbsp extra virgin olive oil
425g/15oz/3¾ cups unbleached strong
white flour
75g/3oz/¾ cup strong wholemeal flour
50g/2oz/⅔ cup freshly grated
Parmesan cheese
7.5ml/1½ tsp salt
10ml/2 tsp granulated sugar
5ml/1 tsp easy-blend dried yeast

LARGE
40g/1½oz/⅓ cup sun-dried tomatoes
240ml/8½fl oz/1¼ cups water
140ml/5fl oz/⅔ cup milk
45ml/3 tbsp extra virgin olive oil
575g/1¼lb/5 cups unbleached strong
white flour
100g/4oz/1 cup strong
wholemeal flour
75g/3oz/1 cup freshly grated
Parmesan cheese
10ml/2 tsp salt
10ml/2 tsp granulated sugar
7.5ml/1½ tsp easy-blend dried yeast

MAKES 1 LOAF

1 Place the tomatoes in a bowl and pour over warm water to cover. Leave to soak for 15 minutes, then tip into a sieve set over a measuring jug (cup). Allow the tomatoes to drain, then chop finely.

2 Check the quantity of tomato water against the amount of water required for the loaf, and add more water if this is necessary. Pour it into the bread machine pan, then add the milk and olive oil. If the instructions for your machine specify that the yeast is to be placed in the pan first, then simply reverse the order in which you add the liquid and dry ingredients.

3 Sprinkle over both types of flour, ensuring that the liquid is completely covered. Sprinkle over the Parmesan, then add the salt and sugar, placing them in separate corners of the bread pan. Make a small indent in the centre of the flour (but not down as far as the liquid) and add the yeast.

4 Set the bread machine to the basic/normal setting; use raisin setting (if available), medium crust. Press Start. Add the tomatoes at the beep or during the last 5 minutes of kneading. Remove the bread at the end of the baking cycle and turn out on to a wire rack to cool.

ROSEMARY AND RAISIN LOAF

*Inspired by a classic Tuscan bread – panmarino – this bread is flavoured
with rosemary and raisins and enriched with eggs and olive oil.*

SMALL
135ml/4½fl oz/⅘ cup water
45ml/3 tbsp extra virgin olive oil
1 egg
*375g/13oz/3¼ cups strong unbleached
white (bread) flour*
*15ml/1 tbsp skimmed milk powder
(non fat dry milk)*
10ml/2 tsp fresh rosemary, chopped
5ml/1 tsp salt
10ml/2 tsp granulated sugar
*5ml/1 tsp easy-blend (rapid-rise)
dried yeast*
75g/3oz/½cup raisins

MEDIUM
160ml/5½fl oz/1 cup water
60ml/4 tbsp extra virgin olive oil
2 eggs
*500g/1lb 2oz/4½ cups unbleached
strong white flour*
30ml/2 tbsp skimmed milk powder
15ml/1 tbsp fresh rosemary, chopped
7.5ml/1½ tsp salt
10ml/2 tsp granulated sugar
5ml/1 tsp easy-blend dried yeast
115g/4oz/generous ⅔ cup raisins

LARGE
200ml/7fl oz/1⅛ cups water
75ml/5 tbsp extra virgin olive oil
3 eggs
*675g/1½lb/6 cups unbleached strong
white flour*
45ml/3 tbsp skimmed milk powder
20ml/4 tsp fresh rosemary, chopped
7.5ml/1½ tsp salt
15ml/1 tbsp granulated sugar
7.5ml/1½ tsp easy-blend dried yeast
150g/5oz/1 cup raisins

MAKES 1 LOAF

1 Pour the water, extra virgin olive oil
and egg(s) into the bread machine pan.
If the instructions for your machine
specify that the yeast is to be placed in
the pan first, then simply reverse the
order in which you add the liquid and
dry ingredients.

2 Sprinkle over the flour, ensuring that
it covers the water. Add the skimmed
milk powder and rosemary. Add the salt
and sugar in separate corners of the
bread pan. Make a small indent in the
centre of the flour (but not down as far
as the liquid) and add the yeast.

3 Set the bread machine to the basic/
normal setting, with raisin setting (if
available), medium crust. Press Start.
Add the raisins when the machine
beeps or 5 minutes before the kneading
cycle ends.

4 Remove the bread at the end of the
baking cycle and turn out on to a wire
rack to cool.

VARIATION
This savoury bread can be made
with chopped almonds and sultanas
(golden raisins) or dried figs, instead
of raisins. All are delicious flavours for
serving with soft cheese.

MIXED HERB COTTAGE LOAF

300ml/10½fl oz/1¼ cups water
450g/1lb/4 cups strong unbleached white
(bread) flour, plus extra for dusting
7.5ml/1½ tsp granulated sugar
7.5ml/1½ tsp salt
7.5ml/1½ tsp easy-blend (rapid-rise)
dried yeast
15ml/1 tbsp chopped fresh chives
10ml/2 tsp chopped fresh thyme
15ml/1 tbsp chopped fresh tarragon
30ml/2 tbsp chopped fresh parsley

For the Glaze
5ml/1 tsp salt

Makes 1 Loaf

There's something very satisfying about the shape of a cottage loaf, and the flavour of fresh herbs – chives, thyme, tarragon and parsley – adds to the appeal. This loaf makes the perfect centrepiece for the table, for guests to help themselves.

1 Pour the water into the bread machine pan. If the operating instructions for your bread machine specify that the yeast is to be placed in the pan first, then simply reverse the order in which you add the water and dry ingredients.

2 Sprinkle over the flour, ensuring that it covers the water completely. Add the granulated sugar and the salt, placing them in separate corners of the bread machine pan. Make a small indent in the centre of the flour (but do not go down as far as the water) and add the easy-blend dried yeast.

3 Set the bread machine to the dough setting; use basic raisin dough setting (if available). Press Start.

4 Add the chives, thyme, tarragon and parsley when the machine beeps to add extra ingredients, or during the final 5 minutes of kneading. Lightly flour two baking sheets.

5 When the dough cycle has finished, remove the dough from the machine. Place it on a surface that has been lightly floured. Knock back (punch down) the dough gently and then divide it into two pieces, making one piece twice as large as the other.

6 Take each piece of dough in turn and shape it into a plump ball. Place the balls of dough on the prepared baking sheets and cover each with a lightly oiled mixing bowl.

7 Leave in a warm place for about 20–30 minutes, or until the dough has almost doubled in size.

8 Cut a cross, about 4cm/1½in across, in the top of the larger piece of dough. Brush the surface with water and place the smaller round on top.

9 Carefully press the handle of a wooden spoon through the centre of both pieces of dough. Cover the loaf with oiled clear film (plastic wrap) and leave it to rise for 10 minutes.

10 Meanwhile, preheat the oven to 220°C/425°F/Gas 7. Mix the salt with 15ml/1 tbsp water in a bowl, then brush the mixture over the top of the bread.

11 Using a sharp knife, make eight long slashes around the top of the bread and 12 small slashes around the base. Dust the top of the bread lightly with strong white flour before placing in the oven.

12 Bake for 30–35 minutes, or until the bread is golden and sounds hollow when tapped on the base. Turn the loaf out on to a wire rack to cool.

VARIATION
Vary the combination of fresh herbs you use, according to availability and taste. You should aim for just under 75ml/5 tbsp in all, but use more pungent herbs sparingly, so they do not become too overpowering.

GRAINY MUSTARD AND BEER LOAF

For a quick, tasty, nutritious and filling lunch, serve chunks of this wonderful bread with cheese and pickles.

COOK'S TIP

Use pale ale for a more subtle taste or brown ale if you prefer a stronger flavour to your bread. Open at least 1 hour before using, to make sure the beer is flat.

1 Pour the beer and oil into the bread machine pan. Add the mustard. If the instructions for your machine specify that the yeast is to be placed in the pan first, reverse the order in which you add the liquid and dry ingredients.

2 Sprinkle over the white and wholemeal flours, ensuring that the liquid is completely covered. Add the skimmed milk powder. Add the salt and sugar, placing them in separate corners of the bread pan. Make a small indent in the centre of the flour (but not down as far as the liquid) and add the yeast.

3 Set the bread machine to the basic/normal setting, medium crust. Press Start.

4 Remove the bread at the end of the baking cycle and turn out on to a wire rack to cool.

GOLDEN PUMPKIN BREAD

*The pumpkin purée gives this loaf a rich golden crumb, a soft crust and a
beautifully moist light texture, as well as a delightfully sweet-savoury flavour.
It is perfect for serving with soups and casseroles.*

1 Mash the cooled pumpkin and put
it in the bread machine pan. Add the
buttermilk, water and oil. If the
instructions for your machine specify
that the yeast is to be placed in the pan
first, reverse the order in which you add
the liquid mixture and dry ingredients.

2 Sprinkle over the flour and maizemeal
(cornmeal), ensuring that the liquid is
completely covered. Add the golden
syrup and salt in separate corners of the
bread machine pan. Make an indent in
the centre of the flour (but not down as
far as the liquid) and add the yeast.

SMALL
150g/5½oz/¾ cup cooked pumpkin
90ml/6 tbsp buttermilk
60ml/4 tbsp/¼ cup water
15ml/1 tbsp extra virgin olive oil
*325g/11½oz/scant 3 cups strong
unbleached white (bread) flour*
50g/2oz/½ cup maizemeal (cornmeal)
15ml/1 tbsp golden (light corn) syrup
5ml/1 tsp salt
*4ml/¾ tsp easy-blend (rapid-rise)
dried yeast*
15ml/1 tbsp pumpkin seeds

MEDIUM
200g/7oz/¾ cup cooked pumpkin
*110ml/scant 4fl oz/scant ½ cup
buttermilk*
45ml/3 tbsp/¼ cup water
30ml/2 tbsp extra virgin olive oil
*425g/15oz/3¾ cups unbleached strong
white flour*
75g/3oz/¾ cup maizemeal
22ml/1½ tbsp golden syrup
7.5ml/1½ tsp salt
5ml/1 tsp easy-blend dried yeast
22ml/1½ tbsp pumpkin seeds

LARGE
250g/9oz/1 cup cooked pumpkin
150ml/5fl oz/⅔ cup buttermilk
80ml/scant 3fl oz/⅓ cup water
45ml/3 tbsp extra virgin olive oil
*575g/1¼lb/5 cups unbleached strong
white flour*
100g/3½oz/scant 1 cup maizemeal
30ml/2 tbsp golden syrup
10ml/2 tsp salt
7.5ml/1½ tsp easy-blend dried yeast
30ml/2 tbsp pumpkin seeds

MAKES 1 LOAF

3 Set the bread machine to the basic/
normal setting; use raisin setting (if
available), medium crust. Press Start.
Add the pumpkin seeds when the
machine beeps, or during the last
5 minutes of kneading.

4 Remove at the end of the baking cycle.
Turn out on to a wire rack to cool.

ROLLS, BUNS AND PASTRIES

These hand-shaped delights include French Petit Pain au Chocolat, Italian Ricotta and

Oregano Knots, and Apple and Sultana Danish Pastries. Chelsea Buns and Devonshire

Splits are British classics, while Parker House Rolls and Doughnuts are traditional American

offerings. Sweet and savoury rolls using mixed grains, herbs, nuts and fruit are just a few

of the characterful small breads to enjoy in this section.

CALAS

50g/2oz/generous ⅓ cup pudding rice
280ml/10fl oz/1¼ cups milk
140ml/5fl oz/⅔ cup water
2 eggs
125g/4½oz/generous 1 cup unbleached strong white (bread) flour
5ml/1 tsp grated lemon rind
2.5ml/½ tsp ground ginger
2.5ml/½ tsp freshly grated nutmeg
50g/2oz/¼ cup sugar
1.5ml/¼ tsp salt
5ml/1 tsp easy-blend (rapid-rise) dried yeast
oil, for deep-frying
icing (confectioners') sugar, for dusting

MAKES ABOUT 25

1 Place the rice, milk and water in a pan and bring to the boil. Lower the heat, cover and simmer for 20 minutes, stirring occasionally. Set aside to cool.

2 Add the eggs to the bread machine pan. Reverse the order in which you add the wet and dry ingredients if necessary.

These tasty morsels are a Creole speciality, made from a rice-based yeast dough which is then deep-fried. They are delicious served warm with coffee or as a breakfast treat.

3 Add the rice. Sprinkle over the flour, then the lemon rind, ginger and nutmeg. Add the sugar and salt, placing them in separate corners of the bread pan. Make a small indent in the centre of the flour (but not down as far as the liquid) and add the yeast.

4 Set the bread machine to the dough setting; use basic dough setting (if available). Press Start. When the dough cycle has finished, lift out the pan containing the batter from the machine.

5 Preheat the oven to 140°C/275°F/Gas 1. Heat the oil for deep-frying to 180°C/350°F or until a cube of dried bread, added to the oil, turns golden in 45 seconds. Add tablespoons of batter a few at a time and fry for 3–4 minutes, turning occasionally, until golden.

6 Use a slotted spoon to remove the calas from the oil and drain on kitchen paper. Keep them warm in the oven while you cook the remainder. When all the calas have been cooked, dust them with icing sugar and serve warm.

COOK'S TIP
If you are using a large bread machine, it is a good idea to make double the quantity of dough. If you use the quantities listed here, it is important to check that all the flour is thoroughly mixed with the liquid.

AMERICAN BREAKFAST PANCAKES

2 eggs
280ml/10fl oz/1¼ cups milk
225g/8oz/2 cups unbleached strong white (bread) flour
5ml/1 tsp salt
15ml/1 tbsp sugar
15g/½oz/1 tbsp butter, melted
5ml/1 tsp easy-blend (rapid-rise) dried yeast
maple syrup or wild cranberry sauce, to serve

MAKES ABOUT 15

1 Separate 1 egg and set the white aside. Place the yolk in the bread machine pan and add the whole egg and the milk. If the instructions for your machine specify that the yeast is to be placed in the pan first, reverse the order in which you add the ingredients.

These thick, succulent breakfast pancakes are often served with a sauce made from wild cranberries, also known as ligonberries. They are equally delicious served with maple syrup and with strips of crispy bacon.

2 Sprinkle over the flour, ensuring that it covers the liquid. Add the salt, sugar and butter, placing them in separate corners of the bread pan. Make a small indent in the centre of the flour (but not down as far as the liquid) and add the easy-blend dried yeast.

3 Set the bread machine to the dough setting; use basic dough setting (if available). Press Start.

4 When the dough cycle has finished pour the batter into a large jug (pitcher). Whisk the reserved egg white; fold it into the batter. Preheat the oven to 140°C/275°F/Gas 1.

5 Lightly oil a large heavy frying pan or griddle and place over a medium heat. Add about 45ml/3 tbsp batter, letting it spread out to form a pancake about 10cm/4in wide. If room, make a second pancake alongside the first.

6 Cook each pancake until the surface begins to dry out, then turn over using a fish slice or spatula and cook the other side for about 1 minute, or until golden.

7 Stack the pancakes between sheets of greaseproof (waxed) paper on a plate and keep them warm in the oven while you cook the rest of the batter. Serve the pancakes with the syrup or sauce.

PETIT PAIN AU CHOCOLAT

A freshly baked petit pain au chocolat is almost impossible to resist, with its buttery, flaky yet crisp pastry concealing a delectable chocolate filling. For a special finish, drizzle melted chocolate over the tops of the freshly baked and cooked pastries.

125ml/4½fl oz/generous ½ cup water
250g/9oz/2¼ cups unbleached strong white (bread) flour
30ml/2 tbsp skimmed milk powder (non fat dry milk)
15ml/1 tbsp sugar
2.5ml/½ tsp salt
140g/5oz/⅔ cup butter, softened
7.5ml/1½ tsp easy-blend (rapid-rise) dried yeast
225g/8oz plain (semisweet) chocolate, broken into pieces

FOR THE GLAZE
1 egg yolk
15ml/1 tbsp milk

MAKES 9

1 Pour the water into the bread machine pan. If the instructions for your bread machine specify that the yeast is to be placed in the pan first, then simply reverse the order of the ingredients.

2 Sprinkle over the flour, then the skimmed milk powder, ensuring that the water is completely covered.

3 Add the sugar, salt and 25g/1oz/ 2 tbsp of the softened butter, placing them in separate corners of the bread pan. Make a small indent in the centre of the flour (but not down as far as the liquid) and add the yeast.

4 Set the breadmaking machine to the dough setting; use basic dough setting (if available). Press Start. Meanwhile shape the remaining softened butter into an oblong-shaped block, about 2cm/¾in thick.

5 Lightly grease two baking sheets. When the dough cycle has finished, place the dough on a floured surface. Knock back (punch down) and shape into a ball. Cut a cross halfway through the top.

6 Roll out around the cross, leaving a risen centre. Place the butter in the centre. Fold the rolled dough over the butter to enclose; seal the edges.

7 Roll to a rectangle 2cm/¾in thick, twice as long as wide. Fold the bottom third up and the top down; seal the edges with a rolling pin. Wrap the dough in lightly oiled clear film (plastic wrap). Chill in the refrigerator for 20 minutes.

8 Do the same again twice more, giving a quarter turn and chilling each time. Chill again for 30 minutes.

9 Roll out the dough to a rectangle measuring 52 × 30cm/21 × 12in. Using a sharp knife, cut the dough into three strips lengthways and widthways to make nine 18 × 10cm/7 × 4in rectangles.

10 Divide the chocolate among the three dough rectangles, placing the pieces lengthways at one short end.

11 Mix the egg yolk and milk for the glaze together. Brush the mixture over the edges of the dough.

12 Roll up each piece of dough to completely enclose the chocolate, then press the edges together to seal.

13 Place the pastries seam side down on the prepared baking sheets. Cover with oiled clear film and leave to rise in a warm place for about 30 minutes or until doubled in size.

14 Meanwhile, preheat the oven to 200°C/400°F/Gas 6. Brush the pastries with the remaining glaze and bake for about 15 minutes, or until golden. Turn out on to a wire rack to cool just slightly and serve warm.

VARIATION
Fill this flaky yeast pastry with a variety of sweet and savoury fillings. Try chopped nuts, tossed with a little brown sugar and cinnamon or, for a savoury filling, thin strips of cheese, wrapped in ham or mixed with chopped cooked bacon.

WHOLEMEAL ENGLISH MUFFINS

*After a long walk on a wintry afternoon, come home to warm muffins,
carefully torn apart and spread thickly with butter.*

350ml/12fl oz/1½ cups milk
*225g/8oz/2 cups unbleached strong
white (bread) flour*
*225g/8oz/2 cups stoneground strong
wholemeal (whole-wheat bread) flour*
5ml/1 tsp sugar
7.5ml/1½ tsp salt
15g/½oz/1 tbsp butter
*7.5ml/1½ tsp easy-blend (rapid-rise)
dried yeast*
rice flour, for dusting

MAKES 9

COOK'S TIP
If you don't have a griddle, cook the
muffins in a heavy frying pan.
It is important that they cook slowly.

1 Pour the milk into the bread machine
pan. If the instructions for your bread
machine specify that the yeast is to be
placed in the pan first, then reverse the
order in which you add the liquid and
dry ingredients.

2 Sprinkle over each type of flour in
turn, making sure that the milk is
completely covered. Add the sugar, salt
and butter, placing each of them in
separate corners of the bread pan. Then
make a small indent in the centre of the
flour (but do not go down as far as the
liquid underneath) and add the easy-
blend dried yeast.

3 Set the machine to the dough setting;
use basic dough setting (if available).
Press Start. Sprinkle a baking sheet
with rice flour.

4 When the dough cycle has finished,
place the dough on a floured surface.
Knock it back gently. Roll out the dough
until it is about 1cm/½in thick.

5 Using a floured 7.5cm/3in plain cutter,
cut out nine muffins. If you like, you can
re-roll the trimmings, knead them
together and let the dough rest for a few
minutes before rolling it out again and
cutting out an extra muffin or two.

6 Place the muffins on the baking sheet.
Dust with rice flour. Cover with oiled
clear film (plastic wrap) and leave to
rise in a warm place for 20 minutes, or
until almost doubled in size.

7 Heat a griddle over a medium heat.
You should not need any oil if the
griddle is well seasoned; if not, add the
merest trace of oil. Cook the muffins
slowly, three at a time, for about
7 minutes on each side. Serve warm.

PARKER HOUSE ROLLS

These stylish rolls were first made in a hotel in Boston, after which they are named. They are delicious served warm.

1 Pour the milk and egg into the bread machine pan. If the instructions for your bread machine specify that the yeast is to be placed in the pan first, reverse the order in which you add the liquid and dry ingredients.

2 Sprinkle over the strong white (bread) flour, ensuring that it covers the liquid. Add the sugar, salt and 25g/1oz/2 tbsp of the melted butter, placing them in separate corners of the pan. Make an indent in the centre of the flour (do not go down as far as the liquid underneath) and add the easy-blend dried yeast.

3 Set the machine to the dough setting; use basic dough setting (if available). Press Start. Lightly oil two baking sheets.

4 When the dough cycle has finished, remove the dough from the machine, place it on a lightly floured surface and knock back (punch down) gently.

180ml/6½fl oz/generous ¾ cup milk
1 egg
450g/1lb/4 cups strong white flour
10ml/2 tsp sugar
7.5ml/1½ tsp salt
75g/3oz/6 tbsp butter, melted
5ml/1 tsp easy-blend (rapid-rise) dried yeast

MAKES 10 ROLLS

COOK'S TIP
If you do not have a small rolling pin – and can't borrow one from a child's cooking set – use a small clean bottle or the rounded handle of a knife to shape the rolls.

5 Roll out to a 1cm/½in thickness. Use a 7.5cm/3in cutter to make ten rounds, then use a small rolling pin to roll or flatten each across the centre in one direction, to create a valley about 5mm/¼in thick.

6 Brush with a little remaining melted butter to within 1cm/½in of the edge. Fold over, ensuring the top piece of dough overlaps the bottom. Press down lightly on the folded edge.

7 Place the rolls on the baking sheets, just overlapping, brush them with more melted butter and cover with oiled clear film (plastic wrap). Leave to rise in a warm place for 30 minutes.

8 Preheat the oven to 200°C/400°F/ Gas 6. Bake the rolls for 15–18 minutes, or until they are golden. Brush the hot rolls with the last of the melted butter and transfer them to a wire rack to cool.

RICOTTA AND OREGANO KNOTS

The ricotta cheese adds a wonderful moistness to these beautifully shaped rolls. Serve them slightly warm to appreciate fully the flavour of the oregano as your butter melts into the crumb.

60ml/4 tbsp ricotta cheese
225ml/8fl oz/scant 1 cup water
450g/1lb/4 cups unbleached strong white (bread) flour
45ml/3 tbsp skimmed milk powder (non fat dry milk)
10ml/2 tsp dried oregano
5ml/1 tsp salt
10ml/2 tsp sugar
25g/1oz/ 2 tbsp butter
5ml/1 tsp easy-blend (rapid-rise) dried yeast

FOR THE TOPPING
1 egg yolk
15ml/1 tbsp water
freshly ground black pepper

MAKES 12

1 Spoon the cheese into the bread machine pan and add the water. Reverse the order of ingredients if necessary.

2 Sprinkle over the flour, ensuring that it covers the cheese and water. Add the skimmed milk powder and oregano. Place the salt, sugar and butter in separate corners of the bread pan. Make a small indent in the centre of the flour (but not down as far as the liquid) and add the yeast.

3 Set the bread machine to the dough setting; use basic dough setting (if available). Press Start. Lightly oil two baking sheets.

4 When the dough cycle has finished, remove the dough from the machine and place it on a lightly floured surface.

5 Knock back (punch down) gently, then divide it into 12 pieces and cover with oiled clear film (plastic wrap).

6 Take one piece of dough, leaving the rest covered, and roll it on the floured surface into a rope about 25cm/10in long. Lift one end of the dough over the other to make a loop. Push the end through the hole in the loop to make a neat knot.

7 Repeat with the remaining dough. Place the knots on the prepared baking sheets, cover them with oiled clear film and leave to rise in a warm place for about 30 minutes, or until doubled in size. Meanwhile, preheat the oven to 220°C/425°F/Gas 7.

8 Mix the egg yolk and water for the topping in a small bowl. Brush the mixture over the rolls. Sprinkle some with freshly ground black pepper and leave the rest plain.

9 Bake for about 15–18 minutes, or until the rolls are golden brown. Turn out on to a wire rack to cool.

WHOLEMEAL AND RYE PISTOLETS

A wholemeal (whole-wheat) and rye version of this French and Belgian speciality. Unless your bread machine has a programme for wholewheat dough, it is worth the extra effort of the double rising, because this gives a lighter roll with a more developed flavour.

290ml/10¼fl oz/1¼ cups water
280g/10oz/2½ cups strong wholemeal (whole-wheat bread) flour
50g/2oz/½ cup unbleached strong white (bread) flour, plus extra for dusting
115g/4oz/1 cup rye flour
30ml/2 tbsp skimmed milk powder (non fat dry milk)
10ml/2 tsp salt
10ml/2 tsp sugar
25g/1oz/2 tbsp butter
7.5ml/1½ tsp easy-blend (rapid-rise) dried yeast

FOR THE GLAZE
5ml/1 tsp salt

MAKES 12

1 Pour the water into the bread pan. If the instructions for your machine specify that the yeast is to be placed in the pan first, reverse the order in which you add the liquid and dry ingredients.

2 Sprinkle over all three types of flour, ensuring that the water is completely covered. Add the skimmed milk powder. Then add the salt, sugar and butter, placing them in separate corners of the bread pan. Make a small indent in the centre of the flour (but do not go down as far as the water underneath) and add the easy-blend dried yeast.

3 Set the bread machine to the dough setting; use wholewheat dough setting (if available). If you have only one basic dough setting you may need to repeat the programme to allow sufficient time for this heavier dough to rise. Press Start. Lightly oil two baking sheets.

4 When the dough cycle has finished, remove the dough from the bread machine pan and place it on a lightly floured surface. Knock back (punch down) gently, then divide the dough into 12 even-size pieces. Cover these with oiled clear film (plastic wrap).

5 Leaving the rest of the dough covered, shape one piece into a ball. Roll on the floured surface into an oval. Repeat with the remaining dough.

6 Place the rolls on the baking sheets. Cover with oiled clear film and leave in a warm place for 30–45 minutes, until almost doubled in size. Preheat the oven to 220°C/425°F/Gas 7.

7 Mix the salt with 5ml/1tbsp water and brush over the rolls. Dust with flour.

8 Using the oiled handle of a wooden spoon held horizontally, split each roll almost in half, along its length. Replace the clear film and leave for 10 minutes.

9 Bake the rolls for 15–20 minutes, until the bases sound hollow when tapped. Turn out on to a wire rack to cool.

HOT CROSS BUNS

The traditional cross on these Easter buns originates from early civilization and probably symbolized the four seasons; it was only later used to mark Good Friday and the Crucifixion.

210ml/7½fl oz/scant 1 cup milk
1 egg
450g/1lb/4 cups unbleached strong white (bread) flour
7.5ml/1½ tsp ground mixed (apple pie) spice
2.5ml/½ tsp ground cinnamon
2.5ml/½ tsp salt
50g/2oz/¼ cup sugar
50g/2oz/¼ cup butter
7.5ml/1½ tsp easy-blend (rapid-rise) dried yeast
75g/3oz/scant ½ cup currants
25g/1oz/3 tbsp sultanas (golden raisins)
25g/1oz/3 tbsp cut mixed (candied) peel

FOR THE PASTRY CROSSES
50g/2oz/½ cup plain (all-purpose) flour
25g/1oz/2 tbsp margarine

FOR THE GLAZE
30ml/2 tbsp milk
25g/1oz/2 tbsp sugar

MAKES 12

1 Add the milk and egg to the bread pan. Reverse the order of ingredients if necessary. Sprinkle over the flour, covering the liquid. Add the mixed spice and cinnamon. Place the salt, sugar and butter in separate corners of the pan.

COOK'S TIP

If preferred, to make the crosses roll out 50g/2oz shortcrust pastry, and cut into narrow strips. Brush the buns with water to attach the crosses.

2 Make a shallow indent in the flour and add the yeast. Set the machine to the dough setting; use basic raisin dough setting (if available). Press Start. Add the dried fruit and peel when the machine beeps or 5 minutes before the end of the kneading period. Meanwhile, lightly grease two baking sheets.

3 When the dough cycle has finished, remove the dough from the machine and place it on a lightly floured surface. Knock back (punch down) gently, then divide it into 12 pieces. Cup each piece between your hands and shape it into a ball. Place on the baking sheets, cover with oiled clear film (plastic wrap) and leave to rise for 30–45 minutes or until the dough has almost doubled in size.

4 Meanwhile, preheat the oven to 200°C/400°F/Gas 6. Make the pastry for the crosses. In a bowl, rub the flour and margarine together until the mixture resembles fine breadcrumbs. Bind with enough water to make a soft pastry which can be piped.

5 Spoon the pastry into a piping (pastry) bag fitted with a plain nozzle and pipe a cross on each bun. Bake the buns for 15–18 minutes, or until golden.

6 Meanwhile, heat the milk and sugar for the glaze in a small saucepan. Stir thoroughly until the sugar dissolves. Brush the glaze over the top of the hot buns. Turn out on to a wire rack. Serve warm or cool.

DEVONSHIRE SPLITS

A summer afternoon, a scrumptious cream tea; Devonshire splits are an essential part of this British tradition.

140ml/5fl oz/⅝ cup milk
225g/8oz/2 cups unbleached strong white (bread) flour
25g/1oz/2 tbsp sugar
2.5ml/½ tsp salt
5ml/1 tsp easy-blend (rapid-rise) dried yeast
icing (confectioners') sugar, for dusting

FOR THE FILLING
clotted or whipped double (heavy) cream
raspberry or strawberry jam

MAKES 8

5 When the dough cycle has finished, remove the dough from the machine and place it on a lightly floured surface.

6 Knock back (punch down) gently, then divide the dough into eight equal-size portions. Shape each portion of dough into a ball, using cupped hands. Place on the prepared baking sheets, and flatten the top of each ball slightly. Cover with oiled clear film (plastic wrap). Leave to rise for 30–45 minutes or until doubled in size.

7 Meanwhile, preheat the oven to 220°C/425°F/Gas 7. Bake the buns for 15–18 minutes, or until they are light golden in colour. Turn out on to a wire rack to cool.

8 Split the buns open and fill them with cream and jam. Dust them with icing sugar just before serving.

2 Sprinkle over the flour, ensuring that it covers all the liquid completely. Then add the sugar and salt, placing them in separate corners of the bread machine pan.

3 Make a small indent in the centre of the flour (do not go down as far as the milk underneath) and pour the easy-blend dried yeast into the hollow.

1 Pour the milk into the bread pan. If your machine instructions specify it, reverse the order in which you add the liquid and dry ingredients.

4 Set the bread machine to the dough setting; use basic dough setting (if available). Press Start. Lightly grease two baking sheets.

DOUGHNUTS

The main thing to remember about doughnuts is the speed with which they disappear, so make plenty of both the cinnamon-coated rings and the round ones filled with jam.

90ml/6 tbsp water
140ml/5fl oz/scant ⅔ cup milk
1 egg
450g/1lb/4 cups unbleached strong white (bread) flour
50g/2oz/¼ cup sugar
5ml/1 tsp salt
50g/2oz/¼ cup butter
7.5ml/1½ tsp easy-blend (rapid-rise) dried yeast
oil for deep-frying
sugar, for sprinkling
ground cinnamon, for sprinkling

FOR THE FILLING
45ml/3 tbsp red jam
5ml/1 tsp lemon juice

MAKES ABOUT 16

1 Pour the water and milk into the bread machine pan. Break in the egg. If the instructions for your bread machine specify that the yeast is to be placed in the pan first, reverse the order in which you add the ingredients.

2 Sprinkle over the flour, ensuring that it covers the liquid. Add the sugar, salt and butter, placing them in separate corners of the bread pan. Make a small indent in the centre of the flour (but not down as far as the liquid) and add the easy-blend dried yeast.

3 Set the bread machine to the dough setting; use basic dough setting (if available). Press Start.

4 When the dough cycle has finished, remove the dough from the machine and place it on a lightly floured surface.

5 Knock back (punch down) gently and divide the dough in half. Cover one half with lightly oiled clear film (plastic wrap). Divide the remaining piece of dough into eight equal portions.

6 Take each portion in turn and use your hands to roll it into a smooth ball. Lightly oil two baking sheets.

7 Place the eight dough balls on one of the prepared baking sheets. Cover them with oiled clear film and leave in a warm place to rise for about 30 minutes, or until doubled in size.

8 Roll the remaining dough out to a thickness of 1cm/½in. Cut into circles using a 7.5cm/3in plain cutter. Then make the dough circles into rings using a 4cm/1½in plain cutter.

9 Place the rings on the remaining baking sheet, cover them with oiled clear film (plastic wrap) and leave them in a warm place for about 30 minutes, or until doubled in size.

10 Heat the oil for deep-frying to 180°C/350°F, or until a cube of dried bread, added to the oil, turns golden brown in 30–60 seconds. Add the doughnuts, three or four at a time.

11 Cook the doughnuts for about 4–5 minutes, or until they are golden. Remove from the oil using a slotted spoon and drain on kitchen paper.

VARIATION
Make oblong shaped doughnuts and split almost in half lengthways once cold. Fill with whipped cream and your favourite jam.

12 Toss the round doughnuts in sugar and the ring doughnuts in a mixture of sugar and ground cinnamon. Set aside to cool.

13 Heat the jam and lemon juice in a small pan until warm, stirring to combine. Leave to cool, then spoon the mixture into a piping (pastry) bag fitted with a small plain nozzle.

14 When the round doughnuts have cooled, use a skewer to make a small hole in each. Insert the piping nozzle and squeeze a little of the jam mixture into each doughnut.

CHELSEA BUNS

225ml/8fl oz/scant 1 cup milk
1 egg
*500g/1lb 2oz/4½ cups unbleached
strong white (bread) flour*
2.5ml/½ tsp salt
75g/3oz/6 tbsp sugar
50g/2oz/¼ cup butter, softened
*5ml/1 tsp easy-blend (rapid-rise)
dried yeast*
25g/1oz/2 tbsp butter, melted
*115g/4oz/⅔ cup sultanas
(golden raisins)*
25g/1oz/3 tbsp chopped candied peel
25g/1oz/2 tbsp currants
25g/1oz/2 tbsp light brown sugar
*5ml/1 tsp ground mixed (apple
pie) spice*

FOR THE GLAZE
50g/2oz/¼ cup sugar
5ml/1 tsp orange flower water

MAKES 12 BUNS

Chelsea buns are said to have been invented by the owner of the Chelsea Bun House in London at the end of the 17th century. They make the perfect accompaniment to a cup of coffee or tea. They are so delicious, it is difficult to resist going back for more!

4 Grease a 23cm/9in square cake tin (pan). When the dough cycle has finished, transfer the dough to a lightly floured surface.

5 Knock back (punch down) gently, then roll out the dough to form a square that is about 30cm/12in.

8 Cover with oiled clear film (plastic wrap). Leave to rise in a warm place for 30–45 minutes, or until the dough slices have doubled in size. Meanwhile preheat the oven to 200°C/400°F/Gas 6.

9 Bake the buns for 15–20 minutes, or until they have risen well and are evenly golden all over. Once they are baked, leave them to cool slightly in the tin before turning them out on to a wire rack to cool further.

10 Make the glaze. Mix the sugar with 60ml/4 tbsp water in a small saucepan. Heat, stirring occasionally, until the sugar is completely dissolved. Then boil the mixture rapidly for 1–2 minutes without stirring, until syrupy.

1 Pour the milk into the bread machine pan. Add the egg. If the instructions for your machine specify that the yeast is to be placed in the pan first, reverse the order in which you add the liquid and dry ingredients.

2 Sprinkle over the flour, ensuring that it completely covers the liquid. Add the salt, sugar and softened butter in three separate corners of the bread machine pan. Make a small indent in the centre of the flour (but not down as far as the liquid) and add the yeast.

3 Set the bread machine to the dough setting; use basic dough setting (if available). Press Start.

6 Brush the dough with the melted butter and sprinkle it with the sultanas, candied peel, currants, brown sugar and mixed spice, leaving a 1cm/½in border along one edge.

7 Starting at a covered edge, roll the dough up, Swiss (jelly) roll fashion. Press the edges together to seal. Cut the roll into 12 slices and then place these cut side uppermost in the prepared tin.

COOK'S TIP
Use icing (confectioners') sugar to make a thin glaze icing to brush over the freshly baked buns.

11 Stir the orange flower water into the glaze and brush the mixture over the warm buns. Serve slightly warm.

90ml/6 tbsp water
1 egg
60ml/4 tbsp/¼ cup Amaretto liqueur
350g/12oz/3 cups unbleached strong
white (bread) flour
30ml/2 tbsp skimmed milk powder
(non fat dry milk)
40g/1½oz/3 tbsp sugar
2.5ml/½ tsp salt
50g/2oz/¼ cup butter, melted
7.5ml/1½ tsp easy-blend (rapid-rise)
dried yeast

FOR THE MARZIPAN FILLING AND TOPPING
115g/4oz/1 cup ground almonds
50g/2oz/½ cup icing
(confectioners') sugar
2–3 drops of almond essence (extract)
1 egg, separated
25ml/5 tsp water
10ml/2 tsp milk
flaked(sliced) almonds, for sprinkling

MAKES 9

1 Pour the water, egg and Amaretto into the bread machine pan. Reverse the order of ingredients if necessary.

2 Sprinkle over the flour, ensuring that it covers the liquid. Add the skimmed milk powder. Place the sugar, salt and butter in separate corners of the bread pan. Make a small indent in the centre of the flour (but not down as far as the liquid) and pour the easy-blend dried yeast into the hollow.

3 Set the bread machine to the dough setting; use basic dough setting (if available). Press Start. Lightly grease two baking sheets and set aside.

MARZIPAN AND ALMOND TWISTS

If you like almonds, you'll love these. Amaretto liqueur, marzipan and flaked almonds make up a triple whammy.

4 Make the marzipan filling. Mix the ground almonds, icing sugar, almond essence, egg white and 15ml/3 tsp of the water in a bowl and set aside. In a separate bowl, beat the egg yolk with the remaining 10ml/2 tsp water.

5 When the dough cycle has finished, remove the dough from the machine and place it on a lightly floured surface. Knock back (punch down) gently and then roll it out into a 45 × 23cm/18 × 9in rectangle. Cut this in half lengthways to make two 23cm/9in squares.

6 Spread the filling over one of the squares to cover it completely. Brush some beaten egg yolk mixture over the remaining square and place it egg-side down on top of the marzipan filling.

7 Cut nine strips, each 2.5cm/1in wide. Cut a lengthways slit near the end of one of the strips. Twist the strip, starting from the uncut end, then pass the end through the slit and seal the ends together, with the egg mixture. Repeat with the remaining strips.

8 Place the twists on the baking sheets and cover with oiled clear film (plastic wrap). Leave in a warm place to rise for 30 minutes or until doubled in size.

9 Meanwhile, preheat the oven to 200°C/400°F/Gas 6. Mix the remaining egg yolk mixture with the milk and brush the mixture over the twists to glaze. Sprinkle with a few flaked almonds and bake for 12–15 minutes, or until golden. Turn out on to a wire rack to cool.

COCONUT MILK SUGAR BUNS

A hint of coconut flavours these spiral-shaped rolls. Serve them warm or cold with butter and preserves.

1 Pour the coconut milk, milk, egg and vanilla essence into the bread machine pan. If the instructions for your bread machine specify that the yeast is to be placed in the pan first, reverse the order in which you add the liquid and dry ingredients to the pan.

2 Sprinkle over the flour, then the coconut, ensuring that the liquid is completely covered. Add the salt, sugar and butter, placing them in separate corners of the bread pan. Make a small indent in the centre of the flour (but not down as far as the liquid underneath) and add the yeast.

3 Set the bread machine to the dough setting; use basic dough setting (if available). Press Start. Then lightly oil two baking sheets.

4 When the dough cycle has finished, transfer the dough to a lightly floured surface. Knock back (punch down) gently. Divide the dough into 12 equal pieces and cover with oiled clear film (plastic wrap).

5 Take one piece of dough, leaving the rest covered; roll it into a rope about 38cm/15in long.

115ml/4fl oz/½ cup canned coconut milk
115ml/4fl oz/½ cup milk
1 egg
2.5ml/½ tsp vanilla essence (extract)
450g/1lb/4 cups unbleached strong white (bread) flour
25g/1oz/⅓ cup desiccated (dry unsweetened shredded) coconut
2.5ml/½ tsp salt
50g/2oz/¼ cup sugar
40g/1½oz/3 tbsp butter
5ml/1 tsp easy-blend (rapid-rise) dried yeast
50g/2oz/¼ cup butter
30ml/2 tbsp demerara (raw) sugar

MAKES 12

6 Curl the rope into a loose spiral on one of the prepared baking sheets. Tuck the end under to seal. Repeat with the remaining pieces of dough, spacing the spirals well apart.

7 Cover the spirals with oiled clear film and leave to rise in a warm place for about 30 minutes, or until doubled in size. Meanwhile, preheat the oven to 220°C/425°F/Gas 7.

8 Melt the butter in a small pan. Brush over the top of the buns and then sprinkle them with the demerara sugar.

9 Place in the oven and bake for about 12–15 minutes, or until the buns are golden and sound hollow when tapped on the base. Turn out on to a wire rack to cool.

APPLE AND SULTANA DANISH PASTRIES

These Danish pastries are filled with fruit and are beautifully light and flaky.

FOR THE DANISH PASTRY
1 egg
75ml/5 tbsp milk
225g/8oz/2 cups unbleached strong
white (bread) flour
15g/½oz/1 tbsp sugar
2.5ml/½ tsp salt
140g/5oz/⅔ cup butter, softened
7.5ml/1½ tsp easy-blend dried yeast

FOR THE FILLING
25g/1oz/2 tbsp butter
350g/12oz cooking apples, diced
15ml/1 tbsp cornflour (cornstarch)
25g/1oz/2 tbsp sugar
30ml/2 tbsp water
5ml/1 tsp lemon juice
25g/1oz/3 tbsp sultanas
(golden raisins)

TO FINISH
1 egg, separated
flaked (sliced) almonds, for
sprinkling

MAKES 12

1 Place the egg and milk in the bread pan. Reverse the order of ingredients if necessary. Sprinkle over the flour. Add the sugar, salt and 25g/1oz/2 tbsp of the butter in separate corners of the pan.

2 Make a shallow indent in the centre of the flour; add the yeast. Set the bread machine to the dough setting; use basic dough setting (if available). Press Start. Lightly oil two baking sheets.

3 Shape the remaining butter into a block 2cm/¾in thick. When the dough cycle has finished, remove the prepared dough and place it on a lightly floured surface. Knock back (punch down) gently and then roll it out into a rectangle that is slightly wider than the butter block, and just over twice as long.

4 Place the butter on one half, fold the pastry over it, then seal the edges, using a rolling pin. Roll the butter-filled pastry into a rectangle 2cm/¾in thick, making it twice as long as it is wide. Fold the top third down and the bottom third up, seal the edges, wrap in clear film (plastic wrap) and chill for 15 minutes. Repeat the folding and rolling twice, giving the pastry a quarter turn each time. Wrap in clear film; chill for 20 minutes.

5 Make the filling. Melt the butter in a pan. Toss the apples, cornflour and sugar in a bowl. Add to the pan and toss.

6 Add the water and lemon juice. Cook over a medium heat for 3–4 minutes, stirring. Stir in the sultanas.

7 Leave the filling to cool. Meanwhile, roll out the pastry into a rectangle measuring 40 × 30cm/16 × 12in. Cut into 10cm/4in squares. Divide the filling among the squares, spreading it over half of each piece of pastry so that when they are folded, they will make rectangles.

8 Brush the pastry edges on each square with the lightly beaten egg white, then fold the pastry over the filling to make a rectangle measuring 10 × 5cm/4 × 2in and press the edges together firmly. Make a few cuts along the long joined edge of each pastry.

9 Place the pastries on the baking sheets, cover them with oiled clear film and leave to rise for 30 minutes.

10 Preheat the oven to 200°C/400°F/ Gas 6. Mix the egg yolk with 15ml/1 tbsp water and brush over the pastries. Sprinkle with a few flaked almonds and bake for 15 minutes, or until golden. Transfer to a wire rack to cool.

APRICOT STARS

When in season these light pastries can be decorated with fresh apricots.

1 quantity Danish pastry – see Apple
and Sultana Danish Pastries

FOR THE FILLING
50g/2oz/½ cup ground almonds
50g/2oz/½ cup icing
(confectioners') sugar
1 egg, lightly beaten
12 drained canned apricot halves

FOR THE GLAZE
1 egg yolk
30ml/2 tbsp water
60ml/4 tbsp apricot jam

MAKES 12

1 Roll out the pastry into a rectangle measuring 40 × 30cm/16 × 12in. Cut into 10cm/4in squares. On each square, make a 2.5cm/1in diagonal cut from each corner towards the centre. Mix the ground almonds, icing sugar and egg together. Divide the filling among the pastry squares, placing it in the centre.

2 Beat the egg yolk for the glaze with half the water. On each square, fold one corner of each cut section to the centre. Secure with the glaze. Place an apricot half, round side up on top in the centre.

3 Lightly oil two baking sheets. Place the pastries on them and cover with oiled clear film (plastic wrap). Leave to rise for 30 minutes until doubled in size. Preheat the oven to 200°C/400°F/Gas 6.

4 Brush the pastries with the remaining egg glaze and bake them for 15 minutes, until golden. While the stars are cooking, heat the apricot jam in a small saucepan with the remaining water. Transfer the cooked pastries on to a wire rack, brush them with the warm apricot glaze and leave to cool.

Yeast Cakes and Teabreads

Rich cakes filled with nuts, spices, dried fruits or chocolate are all part of this diverse range

of breads. A bread machine is the perfect tool for mixing and rising the rich doughs of

Continental specialities, often prepared for special occasions. It's also good for baking

traditional teabreads which combine a light texture and a good flavour. Classic cakes, such

as Coconut Cake and Gingerbread can easily be baked in a bread machine.

90ml/6 tbsp milk
1 egg
225g/8oz/2 cups unbleached strong
white (bread) flour
2.5ml/½ tsp salt
25g/1oz/2 tbsp caster
(superfine) sugar
25g/1oz/2 tbsp butter
5ml/1 tsp easy-blend (rapid-rise)
dried yeast

For the Filling
50g/2oz/½ cup ready-to-eat
dried apricots
15g/½oz/1 tbsp butter
50g/2oz/¼ cup light muscovado
(molasses) sugar
7.5ml/1½ tsp ground cinnamon
2.5ml/½ tsp allspice
50g/2oz/⅓ cup sultanas
(golden raisins)
milk, for brushing

For the Decoration
45ml/3 tbsp icing
(confectioners') sugar
15–30ml/1–2 tbsp orange liqueur
or orange juice
pecan nuts
candied fruits

Serves 8–10

1 Pour the milk and egg into the bread pan. Reverse the order of the wet and dry ingredients if necessary. Sprinkle over the flour. Add the salt, sugar and butter in separate corners of the bread pan. Make a shallow indent in the flour and add the easy-blend dried yeast.

EASTER TEA RING

This Easter tea ring is too good to serve just once a year. Bake it as a family weekend treat whenever you feel self-indulgent. Perfect for a mid-morning coffee break or for tea time.

2 Set the bread machine to the dough setting; use basic dough setting (if available). Press Start. Then lightly oil a baking sheet.

3 When the dough cycle has finished, remove the dough from the bread pan. Place it on a surface that has been lightly floured. Knock back (punch down) gently, then roll it out into a 30 × 45cm/12 × 18in rectangle.

4 Chop the dried apricots into small pieces. Melt the butter for the filling and brush it over the dough. Then sprinkle the dough with the muscovado sugar, ground cinnamon, allspice, sultanas and chopped apricots.

5 Starting from one long edge, roll up the rectangle of dough, as when making a Swiss (jelly) roll. Turn the dough so that the seam is underneath.

6 Curl the dough into a circle, brush the ends with a little milk and seal. Place on the prepared baking sheet.

7 Using a pair of scissors, snip through the circle at 4cm/1½in intervals, each time cutting two-thirds of the way through the dough. Twist the sections so they start to fall sideways.

8 Cover the ring with lightly oiled clear film (plastic wrap) and leave in a warm place for about 30 minutes, or until the dough is well risen and puffy.

9 Preheat the oven to 200°C/400°F/ Gas 6. Bake the Easter tea ring for 20–25 minutes, or until it is golden and well risen. Turn out on to a wire rack and leave to cool slightly.

10 While the tea ring is still warm, make the decoration by mixing together the icing sugar and liqueur or orange juice. Drizzle the mixture over the ring, then arrange pecan nuts and candied fruit on top. Cool completely before serving.

VARIATION
There is a vast range of dried fruits available in the supermarkets. Vary the sultanas and apricots; try dried peaches, mango, melon, cherries and raisins, to name a few. Just make sure that the total quantity stays the same as in the recipe.

MOCHA PANETTONE

*Panettone is the traditional Italian Christmas bread from Milan. This tall
domed loaf is usually filled with dried fruits; for a change try this coffee-
flavoured bread studded with chocolate and pine nuts.*

*30ml/2 tbsp instant coffee powder
140ml/5fl oz/scant ⅔ cup milk
1 egg, plus 2 egg yolks
400g/14oz/3½ cups unbleached strong
white (bread) flour
15ml/1 tbsp (unsweetened)
cocoa powder
5ml/1 tsp ground cinnamon
2.5ml/½ tsp salt
75g/3oz/6 tbsp sugar
75g/3oz/6 tbsp butter, softened
7.5ml/1½ tsp easy-blend (rapid-rise)
dried yeast
115g/4oz plain (semisweet) chocolate
45ml/3 tbsp pine nuts, lightly toasted
melted butter, for glazing*

SERVES 8–10

COOK'S TIP
The dough for this bread is quite
rich and may require a longer rising
time than that provided for by your
bread machine. Check the dough at
the end of the dough cycle. If it does
not appear to have risen very much
in the bread pan, leave the dough in
the machine, with the machine
switched off and the lid closed, for a
further 30 minutes to allow it to rise
to the required degree.

1 In a small bowl, dissolve the coffee
powder in 30ml/2tbsp hot water. Pour
the mixture into the bread machine pan
and then add the milk, egg and egg
yolks. If the instructions for your bread
machine specify that the yeast is to be
placed in the pan first, simply reverse
the order in which you add the liquid
and dry ingredients.

2 Sift the flour and cocoa powder
together. Sprinkle the mixture over the
liquid, ensuring that it is completely
covered. Add the ground cinnamon.
Place the salt, sugar and butter in
separate corners of the bread pan. Make
a small indent in the centre of the flour
(but not down as far as the liquid) and
add the yeast.

3 Set the machine to the dough setting;
use basic dough setting (if available).
Press Start. Lightly oil a 15cm/6in deep
cake tin (pan) or soufflé dish. Using a
double sheet of greaseproof (waxed)
paper that is 7.5cm/3in wider than the
depth of the tin, line the container so
that the excess paper creates a collar.
Meanwhile, roughly chop the chocolate.

4 When the dough cycle has finished,
remove the dough from the machine
and place it on a lightly floured surface.
Knock back (punch down) gently.
Gently knead in the chocolate and pine
nuts and shape it into a ball. Cover it
with lightly oiled clear film (plastic
wrap) and leave it to rest for 5 minutes.

5 Shape the dough into a plump round
loaf which has the same diameter as the
cake tin or soufflé dish, and place in the
base of the container. Cover with oiled
clear film and leave the dough to rise in
a slightly warm place for 45–60 minutes,
or until the dough has almost reached
the top of the greaseproof paper collar.

6 Meanwhile, preheat the oven to 200°C/
400°F/Gas 6. Brush the top of the loaf
with the melted butter and cut a deep
cross in the top. Bake the bread for
about 10 minutes.

7 Reduce the oven temperature to
180°C/350°F/Gas 4 and continue to bake
the panettone for 30–35 minutes more,
or until it is evenly golden all over and
a metal skewer inserted in the centre
comes out clean without any crumb
sticking to it.

8 Leave the panettone in the tin or dish
for 5–10 minutes, then turn out on to a
wire rack and leave it until it is quite
cold before slicing.

RUM AND RAISIN LOAF

Juicy raisins, plumped up with dark rum, flavour this tea-time loaf.
It's more than good enough to serve just as it is, but slices can also be
lightly toasted and buttered as an alternative.

SMALL
75g/3oz/generous ½ cup raisins
22ml/1½ tbsp dark rum
1 egg
140ml/5fl oz/1 cup milk
350g/12oz/3 cups unbleached strong
white (bread) flour
1.5ml/¼ tsp ground ginger
25g/1oz/2 tbsp sugar
2.5ml/½ tsp salt
40g/1½oz/3 tbsp butter
5ml/1 tsp easy-blend (rapid-rise)
dried yeast
10ml/2 tsp clear honey, warmed

MEDIUM
90g/3¼oz/⅔ cup raisins
30ml/2 tbsp dark rum
1 egg
240ml/8½fl oz/1¼ cups milk
500g/1lb 2oz/4½ cups unbleached
strong white flour
2.5ml/½ tsp ground ginger
40g/1½oz/3 tbsp sugar
3.5ml/¾ tsp salt
50g/2oz/¼ cup butter
7.5ml/1½ tsp easy-blend dried yeast
15ml/1 tbsp clear honey, warmed

LARGE
115g/4oz/⅔ cup raisins
45ml/3 tbsp dark rum
2 eggs, lightly beaten
290ml/½pint/1½ cups milk
675g/1½lb/6 cups unbleached strong
white flour
5ml/1 tsp ground ginger
50g/2oz/¼ cup sugar
5ml/1 tsp salt
65g/2½oz/5 tbsp butter
7.5ml/1½ tsp easy-blend dried yeast
15ml/1 tbsp clear honey, warmed

MAKES 1 LOAF

1 Place the raisins and rum in a small bowl and leave to soak for 2 hours. Add the egg(s) and milk to the bread machine pan. If the instructions for your machine specify that the yeast is to be placed in the pan first, reverse the order in which you add the ingredients.

2 Sprinkle over the flour, ensuring that it covers the liquid completely. Add the ground ginger. Add the sugar, salt and butter, placing them in separate corners of the bread machine pan. Make a small indent in the centre of the flour (but not down as far as the liquid) and pour in the dried yeast.

3 Set the bread machine to the basic/normal setting, with raisin setting (if available), medium crust. Press Start. Add the raisins when the machine beeps to add extra ingredients, or after the first kneading.

4 Remove the bread at the end of the baking cycle and turn out on to a wire rack. Brush the top with honey and leave the loaf to cool.

HAZELNUT TWIST CAKE

Easy to make yet impressive, this sweet bread consists of layers of ground nuts, twisted through a rich dough, topped with a maple-flavoured icing.

230ml/8fl oz/1 cup water
1 egg
450g/1lb/4 cups unbleached strong white (bread) flour
45ml/3 tbsp skimmed milk powder (non fat dry milk)
grated rind of 1 orange
2.5ml/½ tsp salt
50g/2oz/¼ cup sugar
75g/3oz/6 tbsp butter, melted
7.5ml/1½ tsp easy-blend (rapid-rise) dried yeast
flaked (sliced) almonds or slivered hazelnuts, to decorate

For the Filling
115g/4oz/1 cup ground hazelnuts
100g/3½oz/scant 1 cup ground almonds
100g/3½oz/scant ½ cup light muscovado (molasses) sugar
2.5ml/½ tsp freshly grated nutmeg
2 egg whites
15ml/1 tbsp brandy

For the Topping
60ml/4 tbsp icing (confectioners') sugar
15ml/1 tbsp hot water
30ml/2 tbsp natural maple syrup

SERVES 6–8

1 Pour the water and egg into the bread pan. Reverse the order in which you add the wet and dry ingredients if necessary.

2 Sprinkle over the flour, covering the liquid. Add the milk powder and orange rind. Place the salt, sugar and butter in separate corners. Make a shallow indent in the centre of the flour, add the yeast.

3 Set the bread machine to the dough setting; use basic dough setting (if available). Press Start. Oil a 23cm/9in springform ring cake tin (pan).

4 When the dough cycle has finished, place the dough on a floured surface. Knock back (punch down) gently, then roll out to a 65 × 45cm/26 × 18in rectangle. Cut in half lengthways.

5 Make the filling by mixing all of the ingredients in a bowl. Divide the filling in half. Spread one portion over each piece of dough, leaving a 1cm/½in clear border along one long edge of each piece.

6 Starting from the other long edge, roll up each piece of dough, Swiss (jelly) roll fashion. Place the two pieces next to each other and twist them together.

7 Brush the ends with a little water. Loop the rope in the tin and gently press the ends together to seal. Cover with lightly oiled clear film (plastic wrap) and leave in a warm place for 30–45 minutes, until risen. Preheat the oven to 200°C/400°F/Gas 6.

8 Bake the cake for 30–35 minutes, or until it is golden and well risen. Leave to cool slightly, then turn the cake out on to a wire rack.

9 Make the icing by mixing the icing sugar, hot water and maple syrup in a bowl. Drizzle over the warm cake. Sprinkle with a few flaked almonds or slivered hazelnuts and leave to cool completely before serving.

MIXED PEEL BRAID

*A succulent citrus filling with a hint of ginger provides the pleasant surprise
in this attractively plaited (braided) coffee-time cake.*

90ml/6 tbsp milk, plus extra for glazing
1 egg
*280g/10oz/2½ cups strong white
(bread) flour*
*5ml/1 tsp ground mixed
(apple pie) spice*
2.5ml/½ tsp salt
25g/1oz/2 tbsp sugar
50g/2oz/¼ cup butter, melted
*5ml/1 tsp easy-blend (rapid-rise)
dried yeast*

FOR THE FILLING
25g/1oz/2 tbsp glacé (candied) ginger
115g/4oz/⅔ cup mixed (candied) peel
50g/2oz/⅓ cup sultanas (golden raisins)
25g/1oz/¼ cup walnut pieces, chopped
45ml/3 tbsp citrus fruit marmalade

FOR THE GLAZE
1 egg yolk
15ml/1 tbsp sugar

SERVES 8

1 Pour the milk and egg into the bread
pan. If necessary, reverse the order of
adding the wet and dry ingredients.

2 Sprinkle over the flour to cover the
liquid. Add the mixed spice. Put the salt,
sugar and butter in separate corners.
Make a small indent in the centre of the
flour and add the yeast.

3 Set the bread machine to the dough
setting; use basic dough setting (if
available). Press Start. Meanwhile lightly
oil a baking sheet and coarsely chop the
glacé ginger.

4 When the dough cycle has finished,
transfer the dough to a lightly floured
surface. Knock back (punch down)
gently, then roll it out to a 28 × 40cm/
11 × 16in rectangle.

5 Make the filling by combining the
ginger, mixed peel, sultanas, walnuts
and marmalade in a bowl. Spread the
mixture lengthways over the middle
third of the rolled-out dough, leaving a
2.5cm/1in border at either end. Using
a sharp knife, cut the two strips of
dough either side of the filling into
diagonal strips angled towards you,
2cm/¾in wide.

6 Working from the far end, fold in the
end piece of dough, then plait (braid)
the dough strips over the filling. Tuck
in the end to seal. Place the braid on the
baking sheet. Cover it with lightly oiled
clear film (plastic wrap) and leave in a
warm place for 30–45 minutes to rise.

7 Preheat the oven to 200°C/400°F/
Gas 6. Make the glaze by mixing the egg
yolk, sugar and about 15ml/1 tbsp milk
in a bowl. Brush the mixture over the
braid. Bake for 10 minutes, then reduce
the oven temperature to 190°C/375°F/
Gas 5 and bake for 10–15 minutes more,
or until the braid is golden and well
risen. Turn out on to a wire rack to cool.

RASPBERRY AND ALMOND TEABREAD

Fresh raspberries and almonds combine perfectly to flavour this mouthwatering cake. Toasted almonds make a crunchy topping.

1 Remove the kneading blade from the bread pan and line the base of the pan with baking parchment or greased greaseproof (waxed) paper.

2 Sift the self-raising flour into a large bowl. Add the butter and rub in with your fingertips until the mixture resembles fine breadcrumbs.

3 Stir in the caster sugar and ground almonds. Gradually beat in the egg(s). If making the small or large teabread, beat in the milk.

4 Fold in the raspberries, then spoon into the pan. Sprinkle over the flaked almonds, if using (see Cook's Tip.)

SMALL
140g/5oz/1¼ cups self-raising (self-rising) flour
70g/2½oz/5 tbsp butter, cut into pieces
70g/2½oz/generous ⅓ cup caster (superfine) sugar
25g/1oz/¼ cup ground almonds
1 egg, lightly beaten
30ml/2 tbsp milk
115g/4oz/1 cup raspberries

MEDIUM
175g/6oz/1½ cups self-raising flour
90g/3½oz/7 tbsp butter, cut into pieces
90g/3½oz/½ cup caster sugar
40g/1½oz/⅓ cup ground almonds
2 eggs, lightly beaten
140g/5oz/1¼ cups raspberries

LARGE
225g/8oz/2 cups self-raising flour
115g/4oz/½ cup butter, cut into pieces
115g/4oz/generous ½ cup caster sugar
50g/2oz/½ cup ground almonds
2 eggs, lightly beaten
45ml/3 tbsp milk
175g/6oz/1½ cups raspberries

MAKES 1 TEABREAD

COOK'S TIP
This cake can be decorated with toasted flaked (sliced) almonds. You will need about 30ml/2 tbsp.

5 Set the bread machine to the "bake only" setting. Set the timer, if possible, for the recommended time. If not, set the timer and check after the shortest recommended time. Bake the small teabread for 35–40 minutes, the medium for 45–50 minutes and the large cake for 65–70 minutes or until well risen.

6 Test by inserting a skewer into the centre of the teabread. It should come out clean. If necessary, bake for a few minutes more. Then remove the pan from the machine. Turn out on to a wire rack to cool after 2–3 minutes.

BANANA AND PECAN TEABREAD

This moist, light teabread is flavoured with banana, lightly spiced with nutmeg and studded with dried fruit and pecan nuts. Weigh the bananas after peeling them – it is important to use the precise quantities given.

SMALL
75g/3oz/6 tbsp butter, softened
150g/5½oz/generous ¾ cup caster
(superfine) sugar
2 eggs, lightly beaten
175g/6oz/1½ cups self-raising
(self-rising) flour, sifted
150g/5½oz peeled ripe bananas
70ml/2½fl oz/5 tbsp buttermilk
1.5ml/¼ tsp baking powder
2.5ml/½ tsp freshly grated nutmeg
100g/3½oz/generous ½ cup sultanas
(golden raisins)
65g/2½oz/generous ½ cup pecan
nuts, chopped
15ml/1 tbsp apricot jam, melted
15ml/1 tbsp banana chips

MEDIUM
100g/3½oz/7 tbsp butter, softened
175g/6oz/⅞ cup caster sugar
2 large (US extra large) eggs,
lightly beaten
200g/7oz/1¾ cups self-raising
flour, sifted
200g/7oz peeled ripe bananas
85ml/3fl oz/6 tbsp buttermilk
2.5ml/½ tsp baking powder
5ml/1 tsp freshly grated nutmeg
125g/4½oz/¾ cup sultanas
75g/3oz/¾ cup pecan nuts, chopped
30ml/2 tbsp apricot jam, melted
30ml/2 tbsp banana chips

LARGE
115g/4oz/½ cup butter, softened
200g/7oz/1 cup caster sugar
3 eggs, lightly beaten
225g/8oz/2 cups self-raising
flour, sifted
225g/8oz peeled ripe bananas
100ml/3½fl oz/7 tbsp buttermilk
2.5ml/½ tsp baking powder
5ml/1 tsp freshly grated nutmeg
140g/5oz/scant 1 cup sultanas
90g/3½oz/scant 1 cup pecan
nuts, chopped
30ml/2 tbsp apricot jam, melted
30ml/2 tbsp banana chips

MAKES 1 TEABREAD

1 Remove the kneading blade from the bread pan and line the base of the pan with baking parchment or greased greaseproof (waxed) paper.

2 Cream the butter and caster sugar in a mixing bowl until pale and fluffy. Gradually beat in the eggs, beating well after each addition, and adding a little of the flour if the mixture starts to curdle.

3 Mash the bananas until completely smooth. Beat into the creamed mixture with the buttermilk.

4 Sift the remaining flour and the baking powder into the bowl. Add the nutmeg, sultanas and pecans; beat until smooth.

5 Spoon into the prepared bread pan. Set the machine to the "bake only" setting. Set the timer, if possible, for the recommended time. If not, set the timer and check the cake after the shortest recommended time. Bake the small or medium cake for 55–60 minutes and the large cake for 65–70 minutes. Test by inserting a skewer in the centre of the teabread. It should come out clean. If necessary, bake for a few minutes more.

6 Remove the pan from the machine. Leave it to stand for about 5 minutes, then turn the cake out on to a wire rack.

7 While the cake is still warm, brush the top with the melted jam and sprinkle over the banana chips. Leave to cool completely before serving.

Peanut Butter Teabread

Peanut butter is used instead of butter or margarine in this tasty teabread, giving it a distinctive flavour and an interesting texture, thanks to the peanut pieces.

1 Remove the kneading blade from the bread pan and line the base of the pan with baking parchment or greased greaseproof (waxed) paper.

2 Cream the peanut butter and sugar in a bowl together until light and fluffy, then gradually beat in the egg(s).

3 Add the milk and flour and mix with a wooden spoon.

COOK'S TIP
Leave a rough finish on the top of the cake before baking to add character.

SMALL
75g/3oz/⅓ cup crunchy peanut butter
65g/2½oz/⅓ cup caster (superfine) sugar
1 egg, lightly beaten
105ml/7 tbsp milk
200g/7oz/1¾ cups self-raising (self-rising) flour

MEDIUM
115g/4oz/⅓ cup crunchy peanut butter
75g/3oz/scant ½ cup caster sugar
1 egg, lightly beaten
175ml/6fl oz/¾ cup milk
300g/10½oz/generous 2¼ cups self-raising flour

LARGE
150g/5½oz/scant ½ cup crunchy peanut butter
125g/4½oz/scant ¾ cup caster sugar
2 eggs, lightly beaten
200ml/7fl oz/⅞ cup milk
400g/14oz/3½ cups self-raising flour

MAKES 1 TEABREAD

4 Spoon the mixture into the bread pan and set the machine to the "bake only" setting. Set the timer, if possible, for the recommended time. If, on your bread machine, the minimum time on the "bake only" setting is for longer than the time suggested here, then set the timer and check the teabread after the shortest recommended time. Bake the small or medium teabread for 45–50 minutes, and the large teabread for 60–65 minutes.

5 The teabread should be well risen and just firm to the touch. Test by inserting a skewer in the centre of the teabread. It should come out clean. If necessary, bake for a few minutes more.

6 Remove the bread pan from the bread machine. Leave it to stand in the pan for 2–3 minutes, then transfer the peanut butter teabread on to a wire rack to cool.

TREACLE, DATE AND WALNUT CAKE

Layered with date purée and finished with a crunchy sugar and walnut topping, this cake is absolutely irresistible.

SMALL

115g/4oz/⅔ cup stoned (pitted) dates
grated rind and juice of ½ lemon
115g/4oz/1 cup self-raising (self-rising) flour
2.5ml/½ tsp each ground cinnamon, ginger and grated nutmeg
50g/2oz/¼ cup butter
50g/2oz/¼ cup light muscovado (molasses) sugar
15ml/1 tbsp treacle (molasses)
30ml/2 tbsp golden (light corn) syrup
40ml/2½ tbsp milk
1 egg
40g/1½oz/⅓ cup chopped walnuts

MEDIUM

140g/5oz/scant 1 cup stoned dates
grated rind and juice of 1 lemon
170g/6oz/1½ cups self-raising flour
3.5ml/¾ tsp each ground cinnamon, ginger and grated nutmeg
75g/3oz/6 tbsp butter
75g/3oz/6 tbsp light muscovado sugar
22ml/1½ tbsp treacle
45ml/3 tbsp golden syrup
60ml/4 tbsp milk
1 large egg
50g/2oz/½ cup chopped walnuts

LARGE

170g/6oz/1 cup stoned dates
grated rind and juice of 1 lemon
225g/8oz/2 cups self-raising flour
5ml/1 tsp each ground cinnamon, ginger and grated nutmeg
115g/4oz/½ cup butter
115g/4oz/½ cup light muscovado sugar
30ml/2 tbsp treacle
60ml/4 tbsp golden syrup
80ml/3fl oz/⅓ cup milk
1 large egg
75g/3oz/¾ cup chopped walnuts

TOPPING FOR ALL SIZES OF LOAF

25g/1oz/2 tbsp butter
50g/2oz/¼ cup light muscovado sugar
22ml/1½ tbsp plain (all-purpose) flour
3.5ml/¾ tsp ground cinnamon
40g/1½oz/⅓ cup chopped walnuts

MAKES 1 CAKE

1 Remove the kneading blade from the bread pan and line the base of the pan with baking parchment or greased greaseproof (waxed) paper. Mix the dates, lemon rind and lemon juice in a saucepan. Add 60ml/4 tbsp of water and bring to the boil, then simmer until soft. Purée in a blender or food processor.

2 Sift the flour and spices together. Cream the butter and sugar until pale and fluffy. Warm the treacle, golden syrup and milk in a pan, until just melted, then beat into the creamed butter mixture. Add the egg and beat in the flour mixture. Stir in the walnuts.

COOK'S TIP

If necessary, increase the quantities of the toppings by 25 per cent for a large cake, or decrease by 25 per cent if you are making a small cake.

3 Place half the mixture in the bread pan. Spread over the date purée, leaving a narrow border of cake mix all round. Top with the remaining cake mixture, spreading it evenly over the date purée.

4 Set the machine to the "bake only" setting. Set the timer, if possible, for the recommended time. If not, set the timer and check after the recommended time. Bake the small cake for 35 minutes, the medium cake for 40 minutes and the large cake for 45 minutes.

5 Mix all of the topping ingredients together. When the cake has baked for the recommended time, sprinkle the topping over and cook for 10–15 minutes more, until the topping starts to bubble and the cake is cooked. Remove the bread pan from the machine. Leave to stand for 10 minutes, then turn out on to a wire rack to cool.

APRICOT, PRUNE AND PEACH TEABREAD

The succulent dried fruits complement the crunchy texture of the hazelnuts and Granary (multi-grain) flour. Serve this unusual fruit bread in slices, either plain or spread thinly with butter.

1 Remove the kneading blade from the bread pan and line the base of the pan with baking parchment or greased greaseproof (waxed) paper.

2 Chop the apricots, prunes and the peaches. Sift the flour, mixed spice and baking powder together into a large bowl. Add the butter and rub in with your fingers until the mixture resembles fine breadcrumbs.

3 Stir in the sugar, apricots, prunes, peaches and hazelnuts. Gradually beat in the milk and egg.

4 Spoon the mixture into the prepared bread pan. Set the machine to the "bake only" setting. Set the timer, if possible, for the recommended time. If not, set the timer and check the cake after the shortest recommended time. Bake the small cake for 40–45 minutes, the medium cake for 45–50 minutes and the large cake for 60–65 minutes, or until well risen and firm to the touch.

5 Test by inserting a skewer in the centre of the teabread. It should come out clean. If necessary, bake for a few minutes more. Then remove the bread pan from the machine. Leave it to stand for 2–3 minutes, then turn the teabread out on to a wire rack to cool.

SMALL
65g/2½oz/generous ¼ cup ready-to-
eat dried apricots
65g/2½oz/generous ¼ cup ready-to-
eat prunes, stoned (pitted)
50g/2oz/¼ cup ready-to-eat
dried peaches
175g/6oz/1½ cups Granary (multi-
grain) flour
5ml/1 tsp ground mixed (apple
pie) spice
7.5ml/1½ tsp baking powder
50g/2oz/¼ cup butter, diced
50g/2oz/4 tbsp light muscovado
(molasses) sugar
40g/1½oz/⅓ cup hazelnuts, halved
100ml/3½fl oz/7 tbsp milk
1 egg, lightly beaten

MEDIUM
75g/3oz/generous ⅓ cup ready-to-eat
dried apricots
75g/3oz/generous ⅓ cup ready-to-eat
prunes, stoned
65g/2½oz/generous ¼ cup ready-to-
eat dried peaches
225g/8oz/2 cups Granary flour
7.5ml/1½ tsp ground mixed spice
10ml/2 tsp baking powder
65g/2½oz/5 tbsp butter, diced
65g/2½oz/5 tbsp light muscovado sugar
50g/2oz/½ cup hazelnuts, halved
150ml/5fl oz/⅔ cup milk
1 egg, lightly beaten

LARGE
100g/3½oz/scant ½ cup ready-to-eat
dried apricots
100g/3½oz/scant ½ cup ready-to-eat
prunes, stoned
75g/3oz/scant ½ cup ready-to-eat
dried peaches
280g/10oz/2½ cups Granary flour
7.5ml/1½ tsp ground mixed spice
12.5ml/2½ tsp baking powder
75g/3oz/6 tbsp butter, diced
75g/3oz/6 tbsp light muscovado sugar
75g/3oz/½ cup hazelnuts, halved
200ml/7fl oz/⅞ cup milk
1 egg, lightly beaten

MAKES 1 TEABREAD

COCONUT CAKE

Desiccated coconut gives this simple, speedy cake a wonderful moist texture and delectable aroma.

SMALL
75g/3oz/6 tbsp butter, softened
115g/4oz/generous ½ cup caster (superfine) sugar
2 eggs, lightly beaten
115g/4oz/1⅓ cups desiccated (dry unsweetened shredded) coconut
85g/3oz/¾ cup self-raising (self-rising) flour
55ml/2fl oz/¼ cup sour cream
5ml/1 tsp grated lemon rind

MEDIUM
100g/3½oz/7 tbsp butter, softened
140g/5oz/¾ cup caster sugar
2 large eggs, lightly beaten
140g/5oz/1⅔ cups desiccated coconut
100g/3½oz/scant 1 cup self-raising flour
70ml/2½fl oz/scant ⅓ cup sour cream
7.5ml/1½ tsp grated lemon rind

LARGE
115g/4oz/½ cup butter, softened
175g/6oz/scant 1 cup caster sugar
3 eggs, lightly beaten
175g/6oz/2 cups desiccated coconut
115g/4oz/1 cup self-raising flour
85ml/3fl oz/⅜ cup sour cream
10ml/2 tsp grated lemon rind

MAKES 1 CAKE

1 Remove the kneading blade from the bread pan and line the base of the pan with baking parchment or greased greaseproof (waxed) paper.

2 Cream the butter and sugar together until pale and fluffy, then add the beaten eggs a little at a time, beating well after each addition.

3 Add the desiccated coconut, flour, sour cream and lemon rind. Gradually mix together, using a non-metallic spoon.

4 Spoon into the pan. Set the machine to the "bake only" setting. Set the timer, if possible, for the recommended time. If not, set the timer and check after the shortest recommended time. Bake the small or medium cake for 45–50 minutes and the large cake for 65–70 minutes.

5 Test by inserting a skewer into the centre of the cake. It should come out clean. If necessary, bake for a few minutes more.

6 Remove the bread pan from the machine. Let stand for 2–3 minutes, then turn the cake out on to a wire rack to cool.

COOK'S TIP
This is delicious with a lemon syrup drizzled over the cooked cake. Heat 30ml/2 tbsp lemon juice with 100g/3½oz/scant ½ cup granulated sugar and 85ml/3fl oz/6 tbsp water in a saucepan, stirring until the sugar has dissolved. Bring to the boil, then simmer for 2–3 minutes before drizzling the syrup over the warm coconut cake.

GINGERBREAD

—

This tea-time favourite can be baked easily in your bread machine. Store it in an airtight container for a couple of days to allow the characteristic moist sticky texture to develop fully.

1 Remove the blade from the bread pan and line the base with baking parchment or greased greaseproof (waxed) paper. Drain and finely chop the stem ginger. Meanwhile sift all of the dry ingredients together into a large bowl.

2 Melt the sugar, butter, syrup and treacle in a saucepan over a low heat.

3 Make a well in the centre of the dry ingredients and pour in the melted mixture. Add the milk, egg and stem ginger and mix thoroughly.

4 Pour the mixture into the bread pan and set the machine to the "bake only" setting. Set the timer, if possible, for the recommended time. If not, set the timer and check the gingerbread after the shortest recommended time. Bake the small gingerbread for 45–50 minutes, the medium for 50–55 minutes and the large for 65–70 minutes, or until well risen.

5 Remove the bread pan from the machine. Let stand for 2–3 minutes, then turn the gingerbread out on to a wire rack to cool.

SMALL
40g/1½oz/¼ cup bottled stem
(preserved) ginger
175g/6oz/1½ cups plain (all-
purpose) flour
3.5ml/¾ tsp ground ginger
5ml/1 tsp baking powder
1.5ml/¼ tsp bicarbonate of soda
(baking soda)
2.5ml/½ tsp ground mixed (apple
pie) spice
75g/3oz/6 tbsp light muscovado
(molasses) sugar
50g/2oz/¼ cup butter, cut into pieces
75g/3oz/scant ¼ cup golden (light
corn) syrup
40g/1½oz/3 tbsp black treacle
(molasses)
105ml/7 tbsp milk
1 egg, lightly beaten

MEDIUM
50g/2oz/⅓ cup bottled stem ginger
225g/8oz/2 cups plain flour
5ml/1 tsp ground ginger
7.5ml/1½ tsp baking powder
2.5ml/½ tsp bicarbonate of soda
2.5ml/½ tsp ground mixed spice
115g/4oz/½ cup light
muscovado sugar
75g/3oz/6 tbsp butter, cut into pieces
100g/3½oz/¼ cup golden syrup
50g/2oz/4 tbsp black treacle
150ml/5fl oz/⅔ cup milk
1 egg, lightly beaten

LARGE
50g/2oz/⅓ cup bottled stem ginger
280g/10oz/2½ cups plain flour
7.5ml/1½ tsp ground ginger
10ml/2 tsp baking powder
3.5ml/¾ tsp bicarbonate of soda
3.5ml/¾ tsp ground mixed spice
125g/4½oz/generous ½ cup light
muscovado sugar
115g/4oz/½ cup butter, cut into pieces
125g/4½oz/scant ½ cup golden syrup
50g/2oz/4 tbsp black treacle
200ml/7fl oz/⅞ cup milk
1 egg, lightly beaten

MAKES 1 LOAF

POLISH BABKA

60ml/4 tbsp vodka
2.5ml/½ tsp saffron strands
15ml/1 tbsp grated orange rind
15ml/1 tbsp grated lemon rind
115g/4oz/½ cup butter, softened
75g/3oz/6 tbsp caster
(superfine) sugar
3 eggs
30ml/2 tbsp water
400g/14oz/3½ cups unbleached strong
white (bread) flour
2.5ml/½ tsp salt
10ml/2 tsp easy-blend (rapid-rise)
dried yeast
75g/3oz/½ cup raisins
75g/3oz/½ cup dried sour cherries

FOR THE ICING
115g/4oz/1 cup icing (confectioners')
sugar
15ml/1 tbsp lemon juice

FOR THE DECORATION
toasted flaked (sliced) almonds
candied orange peel

SERVES 8–10

*Vodka is the surprise ingredient in this classic Polish cake, made at
Eastertime. The dough is enriched with eggs and flavoured with
citrus peel and raisins.*

1 Steep the vodka, saffron and citrus rinds together for 30 minutes. Beat the butter and sugar until pale and creamy. Tip the saffron mixture into the bread pan, then add the eggs and water. If necessary, reverse the order.

2 Add the flour. Add the salt in a corner. Make an indent; add the yeast. Set to the dough setting; use basic raisin dough setting (if available). Press Start.

3 Mix for 5 minutes, then add the creamed butter and sugar mixture.

4 Tip in the raisins and dried sour cherries when the machine beeps, or 5 minutes before the end of the kneading cycle. Lightly oil a brioche tin (pan). When the cycle has finished, transfer the dough to a floured surface.

5 Knock back (punch down) gently, and shape it into a plump round ball. Place the dough in the tin, cover with lightly oiled clear film (plastic wrap) and leave in a warm place for 2 hours, or until it has risen almost to the top of the tin.

6 Preheat the oven to 200°C/400°F/Gas 6. Bake the babka for 20 minutes. Reduce the oven temperature to 190°C/375°F/Gas 5 and continue to bake for 15–20 minutes more, until golden.

7 Turn the babka out on to a wire rack to cool. Meanwhile, make the icing. Place the icing sugar in a small bowl and add the lemon juice and 15ml/1 tbsp hot water. Mix well, then drizzle the icing over the cake. Sprinkle over the toasted almonds and candied orange peel to decorate.

STRAWBERRY TEABREAD

Perfect for a summertime treat, this hazelnut-flavoured teabread is laced with luscious fresh strawberries.

SMALL
115g/4oz/1 cup strawberries
115g/4oz/½ cup butter, softened
115g/4oz/generous ½ cup caster
(superfine) sugar
2 eggs, beaten
140g/5oz/1¼ cups self-raising
(self-rising) flour, sifted
25g/1oz/¼ cup ground hazelnuts

MEDIUM
170g/6oz/1½ cups strawberries
140g/5oz/⅔ cup butter, softened
140g/5oz/¾ cup caster sugar
2 eggs, beaten
15ml/1 tbsp milk
155g/5½oz/1⅓ cups self-raising
flour, sifted
40g/1½oz/⅓ cup ground hazelnuts

LARGE
200g/7oz/1¾ cups strawberries
175g/6oz/¾ cup butter, softened
175g/6oz/⅞ cup caster sugar
3 eggs, beaten
175g/6oz/1½ cups self-raising
flour, sifted
50g/2oz/½ cup ground hazelnuts

MAKES 1 TEABREAD

1 Remove the kneading blade from the bread pan and line the base of the pan with baking parchment or greased greaseproof (waxed) paper.

2 Hull the strawberries and chop them roughly. Set them aside. Cream the butter and sugar in a mixing bowl until pale and fluffy.

3 Gradually beat in the eggs and milk (if you are making the medium cake), beating well after each addition to combine quickly without curdling.

4 Mix the self-raising flour and the ground hazelnuts together and gradually fold into the creamed mixture, using a metal spoon.

5 Fold in the strawberries and spoon the mixture into the bread pan. Set the machine to the "bake only" setting. Set the timer, if possible, for the recommended time. If, on your bread machine, the minimum time is longer than the time suggested here, set the timer and check after the shortest recommended time. Bake the small or medium teabread for 45–50 minutes and the large teabread for 55–60 minutes.

6 Test by inserting a skewer in the centre of the teabread. It should come out clean. If necessary, bake for a few minutes more.

7 Remove the bread pan from the machine. Leave the teabread to stand for 2–3 minutes, then turn out on to a wire rack to cool.

UK
MANUFACTURERS

PRIMA INTERNATIONAL
4 Elland Park Industrial Estate
Elland Way
Leeds LS11 0EY
Tel: 0113 251 1500
www.prima–international.com

PANASONIC
Panasonic House
Willoughby Road, Bracknell
Berks RG12 8FP
Tel: 01344 862 444

PIFCO
Failsworth
Manchester M35 0HS
Tel: 0161 947 3000
Brand: Russell Hobbs

HINARI
Harvard House
14–16 Thames Road, Barking
Essex IG11 0HX
Tel: 020 8787 3111

PULSE HOME PRODUCTS LTD
Vine Mill, Middleton Road
Royton
Oldham OL2 5LN
Tel: 0161 652 1211
Helpline: 0800 525 089
Brand: Breville

FLOURS

DOVE FARM FOODS LTD
Salisbury Road, Hungerford
Berkshire RG17 0RF
01488 684 880

WEST MILL FOODS LTD
10 Dane Street, Bishop's Stortford
Hertfordshire CM23 3XS
Tel: 01279 658 473
Brand: Allinson

RETAILERS
The following retailers sell bread machines in many of their branches, but ring for details of your local store and the brands of available.

ALLDERS   Helpline: 0800 528 7000
ARGOS   Helpline: 0870 600 3030
COMET   Helpline: 0845 600 7002
CURRYS   Helpline: 0500 304 304
DEBENHAMS
    Head office tel: 020 7408 4444
HOUSE OF FRASER Check a telephone book for details of local stores
JENNERS   Tel: 0131 225 2442
    Princes Street, Edinburgh
JOHN LEWIS PARTNERSHIP Check a telephone book for local stores
MILLER BROTHERS
    Head office tel: 01302 321 333
SCOTTISH POWER
    Helpline: 0800 027 3322
SELFRIDGES Tel: 020 7629 1234
    Oxford Street, London
TEMPO   Helpline: 0870 543 5363

UNITED STATES
MANUFACTURERS

APPLIANCE CO. OF AMERICA
P.O. Box 220709
Great Neck, NY 11021
Tel: (800) 872-1656

BREADMAN (subsidiary of Salton)
www.salton-maxim.com

OSTER
www.oster.com

PANASONIC
www.prodcat.panasonic.com/shop

Toastmaster (subsidiary of Salton)
www.salton-maxim.com

WEST BEND HOUSEWARES
www.westbend.com/house.html

ZOJIRUSHI
www.zojirushi.com/bread.html

RETAILERS
DEAN & DELUCA
110 Greene Street
Suite 304
New York, NY 10012
Tel: (800) 221-7714

JCPENNEY
www.jcpenney.com

MACY'S
www.macys.com

WILLIAMS-SONOMA
P.O. Box 7456
San Francisco, CA 94120-7456
Tel: (800) 541-2233

ARROWHEAD MILLS
P.O. Box 866
Hereford, TX 79045
Tel: (806) 364-0730

BOB'S RED MILL
5209 S.E. International Way
Milwaukie, OR 97222
Tel: (503) 654-3215

CATHY'S COUNTRY STORE
2125 N. Richmond Street
Appleton, WI 54911
(920) 830-3311

KENYON CORNMEAL COMPANY
Osquepough, RI 02836
Tel: (401) 783-4054

KING ARTHUR FLOUR
P.O. Box 876
Norwich, VT 05055-0876
Tel: (800) 827-6836
www.kingarthur.com

WALNUT ACRES ORGANIC FARMS
Penns Creek, PA 17862
Tel: (800) 433-3998

THE CHEF'S CATALOGUE
3215 Commercial Avenue
Northbrook, IL 60062-1900
Tel: (800) 338-3232

BREAD BAKER'S GUILD OF AMERICA
P.O. Box 22254
Pittsburgh, PA 15222
Tel: (412) 322-8275

AUSTRALIA
ADELAIDE

MYER
22 Rundle Mall, Adelaide
(08) 8205 9111

HARVEY NORMAN
822 Marion Road, Marion
(08) 8375 7777

BRISBANE
CHANDLERS
Shop 88, Myer Centre
Queen Street, Brisbane
(07) 3221 2011

BETTA ELECTRICAL
6 Victoria Street
Celvin Grove, Brisbane
(07) 3831 0950

MELBOURNE
DAIMARU CNR
Elizabeth St and Swanson Walk
(03) 9660 6666

RETRAVISION
310 Clarendon Street
South Melbourne
(03) 9699 4577

PERTH
HARVEY NORMAN
1363 Albany Highway, Cannington
(08) 9311 1100

MYER
Murray Street, Perth
(08) 9221 3444

SYDNEY
DAVID JONES
Elizabeth Street, Sydney
(02) 9266 5544

GRACE BROS
436 George Street, Sydney
(02) 9238 9111

BING LEE
Shop 1, HIA Building & Renovation
    Supa Centre, Homebush
(02) 9763 5077

USEFUL HOTLINES
WESTON MILLING   Tel: 1800 649 494
BREVILLE   Tel: 1800 807 911
PANASONIC   Tel: 13 26 00
SUNBEAM   Tel: 1800 025 059
RONSON   Tel: 1800 654 614

The publishers would like to
thank the following companies
who lent equipment and flours:
Prima International
Panasonic
PIFCO
Hinari
Pulse Home Products Ltd
West Mill Foods Ltd
Dove Farm Foods Ltd
Magimix

NOTES

NOTES